Contents

Pathways Plus

Strategic Management and Leadership

Level 7

Unit 7003

Financial management

Pathways Plus

Unit 7003: Financial management

Copyright © Chartered Management Institute, Management House, Cottingham Road, Corby, Northants NN17 1TT.

First edition 2009

Authors:	Bill Snaith and Jane Walker, Durham Business School
Consultant:	Bob Croson
Series consultant:	Roger Merritt Associates
Project manager:	Trevor Weston
Editor:	Suzanne Pattinson
Page layout by:	Decent Typesetting

British Library Cataloguing-in-Publication Data. A CIP catalogue record for this publication is available from the British Library.

ISBN 0-85946-336-2

Every effort has been made to trace holders of copyright material reproduced here. In cases where this has been unsuccessful or if any have inadvertently been overlooked, the publishers will be pleased to address this at the first opportunity.

The publisher would like to thank the following for permission to reproduce copyright material:

- Figure 2.1a on p. 56 has been taken from Atrill, P. and McLaney, E. *Management Accounting for Decision Makers* (2007) published by Pearson Education.

About Pathways Plus

Development guides

There are 12 development guides in the *Pathways Plus* series to cover the 14 units of the qualifications at CMI Level 7: Strategic Management and Leadership.

7001   Personal development as a strategic manager
(ISBN: 0-85946-326-5)

7002   Strategic performance management
(ISBN: 0-85946-331-1)

7003   Financial management
(ISBN: 0-85946-336-2)

7004   Strategic information management
(ISBN: 0-85946-341-9)

7005   Conducting a strategic management project
(ISBN: 0-85946-346-X)

7006/   Organisational direction and strategic planning
7011   (ISBN: 0-85946-351-6)

7007   Financial planning
(ISBN: 0-85946-356-7)

7008   Strategic marketing
(ISBN: 0-85946-361-3)

7009   Strategic project management
(ISBN: 0-85946-340-0)

7010   Organisational change
(ISBN: 0-85946-345-1)

7012   Human resource planning
(ISBN: 0-85946-350-8)

7013/   Being a strategic leader and strategic leadership practice
7014   (ISBN: 0-85946-355-9)

For further details on the development guides:

- Phone: (+44) (0)1536 207344
- Fax: (+44) (0)1536 207384
- Email: publications@managers.org.uk

Qualification structure

There are three qualifications available:

- **CMI Level 7 Award in Strategic Management and Leadership**

  Candidates need to complete any combination of units to a minimum of 6 credits to achieve the qualification.

- **CMI Level 7 Certificate in Strategic Management and Leadership**

  Candidates need to complete any combination of units to a minimum of 13 credits to achieve the qualification.

- **CMI Level 7 Diploma in Strategic Management and Leadership**

  Candidates need to complete all core units (Group A) and three optional units (Group B) to a total of at least 66 credits to achieve the qualification.

Units	Credit
Group A	
Unit 7001 Personal development as a strategic manager	6
Unit 7002 Strategic performance management	7
Unit 7003 Financial management	7
Unit 7004 Strategic information management	9
Unit 7005 Conducting a strategic management project	10
Unit 7006 Organisational direction	9
Group B	
Unit 7007 Financial planning	6
Unit 7008 Strategic marketing	6
Unit 7009 Strategic project management	6
Unit 7010 Organisational change	7
Unit 7011 Strategic planning	9
Unit 7012 Human resource planning	8
Unit 7013 Being a strategic leader	7
Unit 7014 Strategic leadership practice	7

How to use the development guides

The development guides provide a critical commentary to the ideas of writers and thinkers in the management and leadership field. They offer opportunities for you to investigate and apply these ideas within your working environment and job role.

Structure

Each guide is divided into sections that together cover the knowledge and understanding required for the equivalent unit or units of the Chartered Management Institute Level 7 Strategic Management and Leadership qualifications.

Each section starts with a clear set of objectives linked to the learning outcomes of the qualification. You don't have to complete the sections in the order they appear in the guide (the mind map at the beginning of each guide will help you decide which sections and topics are of particular need or interest) but you should try to cover all sections if you are aiming for a full diploma qualification.

Activities

Throughout the guides there are activities for you to complete. These activities are designed to help you reflect on your own situation and apply your research to your organisation. Space and tables are provided within the activities for you to enter your own thoughts or findings, but in some cases you may choose to copy out the table or make notes in a separate notebook.

Timings

Timings are suggested for each activity to give you a rough idea of how long you should devote to them. They're not hard and fast and you must decide whether you will benefit from spending longer on some activities than stated.

Supporting resources

The text of the guides is designed to provide you with an introduction to the subject and a commentary on some of the key issues, models and thinkers in the field. The activities are there to help provide a framework for your thinking. A key component of *Pathways Plus* (*Pathways Plus* because the development guides work together with the online supporting resources to provide an overall learning journey) is the list of references given throughout the text and at the end of each topic guiding you to the most appropriate supporting resources for you to explore yourself. These are marked with the symbol **SR** (as shown above).

You have the opportunity to select those resources that are of most interest or relevance to you and to use them as a source of guided research on a particular topic. Many of the supporting resources are immediately available by logging into CMI's online

P+ Student Resource Centre (SRC) or the CMI online management and leadership portal, ManagementDirect(MDir), whichever you have access to. These resources are marked in the reference list at the end of each topic with **P+** standing for *Pathways Plus*. A button on the first page of the site (whether SRC or MDir) will take you straight to the list of supporting resources as listed in the *Pathways Plus* topics. When there, click on the title of your development guide, the section and the topic you're interested in and then click straight to the article, video, podcast, checklist, extract or report that you want to find.

For those resources that are not available through the CMI site, you will be directed to other sources (some also online) to reach what you need.

Preparing for assessment

Further information on assessment is available in the Student Guide produced as part of the *Pathways Plus* series. If you have any further questions about assessment procedures, it's important that you resolve these with your tutor or centre coordinator as soon as possible.

Further reading

You will find suggestions for further reading at the end of this guide as well as in the Student Resource Centre section of the Institute website at www.managers.org.uk/students.

Alternatively, email mic.enquiries@managers.org.uk or telephone 01536 207400.

Introduction

Welcome to this development guide on financial management. We suggest that you approach this guide with the following key thoughts:

- There's no such thing as 'finance' — just a financial impact of management decisions and actions.

- Managers like yourself don't need to be accountants, but you do need to understand the financial consequences of your decisions, analyse and interpret financial information and be able to communicate with financial experts.

- Financial management is based on numbers that can act as indicators or comparators against previous or expected performance — even a competitor's performance. But these need to be interpreted carefully in order to ensure indications do not become accepted as reality.

- Professional book-keeping ensures that validated data produces reliable information. You should therefore feel comfortable that any financial analysis you do, or decisions you make based on financial information you receive, is built on solid foundations.

SR 2 To complete this guide you should have a basic understanding and awareness of financial statements. If you've done the Level 5 qualification (Unit 5007 *Financial control*) you should have a good enough basic knowledge. If you haven't done a previous qualification that includes finance you could either refer to Unit 5007 or rely more on the Supporting resources lists given at the end of each topic in this guide.

The guide predominantly uses financial terminology that relates to the private sector. We recognise that many people using this guide will be working in the public sector, but as the two sectors are moving closer together this approach should be appropriate.

The guide is split into three sections. In the first section you will look at analysing financial data. Then in the second section you go on to look at the issue of ensuring that budgets meet organisational objectives. In the third, and final, section you look at how you can best evaluate financial proposals. This follows the sequence of the learning outcome for this unit.

This guide has links to other guides, in particular 7007 *Financial planning* and 7004 *Strategic information management*.

Development guide mind map

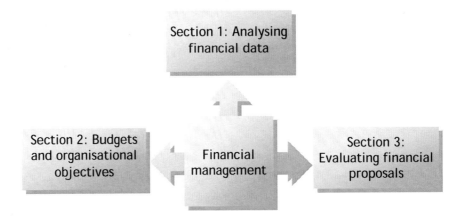

Assessment

If you're studying for the Level 7 in Strategic Management and Leadership qualifications you will be assessed by your approved centre on your knowledge and understanding of the following learning outcomes:

Unit 7003:

1   Be able to assess financial data

2   Be able to assess budgets based on financial data to support financial objectives

3   Be able to evaluate financial proposals for expenditure submitted by others

Section 1 Analysing financial data

Introduction

As analysing financial data is likely to be a new subject to many, an accessible approach is to look at the subject in a very structured way, mirroring the assessment criteria for this qualification:

- Determine how to obtain financial data and assess its validity

- Apply different types of analytical tools and techniques to a range of financial documents and formulate conclusions about performance levels and needs of stakeholders

- Conduct comparative analysis of financial data

- Review and question financial data.

With this structured approach you should gain an understanding of the role of financial data at the appropriate level, and be able to prove that understanding at assessment.

Learning outcomes

This section covers the following learning outcome:

7003.1   Be able to analyse financial data

Section mind map

There are four topics in this section, as shown below. Check the subjects within each one and then continue with the areas you need to explore.

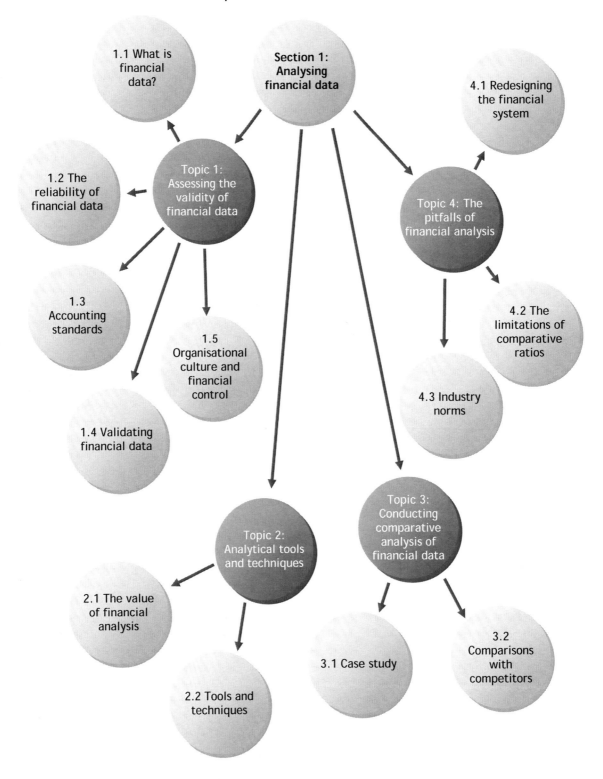

Topic 1:   Assessing the validity of financial data

Introduction

This topic introduces financial data capture, processing and assuring validity.

Financial data is derived from many sources, processed in many ways and used by many people. Unfortunately, this means that there are many chances for error! Capturing the right data at the right time, processing it reliably and correctly and then sharing it in a timely fashion with the right people is fundamental to an organisation's financial control.

Organisations often have to decide between timeliness and accuracy. Taking too long to capture and process accurate data may mean that it reaches the decision makers too late. A balance is always necessary in order to gain the maximum benefit in a timely manner.

The validity of financial data is whether the data measures what it's supposed to measure, which is crucial to making well-informed decisions in any organisation.

1.1   What is financial data?

First, you need to consider the role of data in general, its transformation into information, and its combination into knowledge inside your organisation. This progressive flow can be represented as follows:

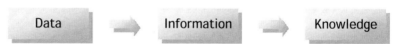

This flow shows that if you don't get step one right, then at best steps two and three are limited — and at worst they are actually flawed. This can result in misinformation, incorrect knowledge and ill-informed decisions. This is also true of financial data — 'Garbage in = Garbage out' (the GIGO principle).

For financial data you also need to distinguish between internal and external sources.

Internal sources of financial data	External sources of financial data
Your accounting system	Companies House
Other managers	The web (many public sector organisations use this as a means of keeping the public informed)
Directly from your suppliers	
Directly from your customers	
Numerous personal spreadsheets	Databases of financial information
	Libraries
	Research documents

SR 16

You should consider conducting an information audit to ascertain what is, and what could be, available inside your organisation.

Activity

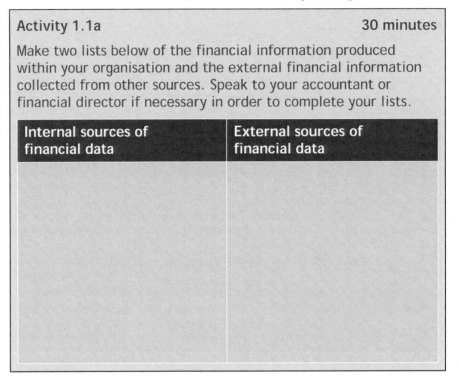

Activity 1.1a	30 minutes

Make two lists below of the financial information produced within your organisation and the external financial information collected from other sources. Speak to your accountant or financial director if necessary in order to complete your lists.

Internal sources of financial data	External sources of financial data

There's no absolute answer for the internal or external sources of data that each organisation should have, but this activity should have helped you find out what's available and what kinds of data your organisation might need to generate or get hold of.

1.2 The reliability of financial data

For the purpose of this subject you're going to focus on the major sources of information. (You will find one of the terms in this box, GAAP, explained in greater detail later in the topic.)

Source of financial data	Indicators of reliability
Your accounting system	Can be influenced by: ■ internal audit ■ financial systems design ■ internal checks and controls ■ authority levels ■ complexity of the accounting system ■ complexity of financial reports ■ the culture of the organisation regarding importance of finance
Example: If an organisation has strict controls over purchase requisitions and purchase orders, yet gives the most junior member of the team the job of allocating account and cost-centre codes then errors may still occur in the processing of the financial data.	

Source of financial data	Indicators of reliability
Published accounts	Can be influenced by: ■ accounting standards ■ auditing standards ■ interpretation of the generally accepted accounting principles (GAAP) ■ accounting statement formats ■ nationality of parent company ■ the auditing/accounting firm employed
	Example: A major variant in reporting in published accounts relates to the treatment of profit and depreciation. Some accounting statements refer to profit for operating activities which includes the cost of depreciation. Other systems talk about EBITDA (Earnings Before Interest, Tax, Depreciation and Amortisation), which treats depreciation as an item worthy of independent reporting.
Published sources of comparative financial information	Can be influenced by: ■ the approach of the publisher to standardising the financial statements ■ the accuracy of the translation from published data into the preferred format
	Example: The format of the balance sheet in the Keynote publication follows the IFAC standard.

Activity

Activity 1.2a   45 minutes

Get hold of the published accounts of one of your competitors (or another similar company to your own). Look at the format of your published accounts and compare the layout with the accounts of the other company. What similarities and differences are there?

As a comparison, you could look at the IFRS Illustrative Financial Statements published in July 2008.

For public sector organisations you may want to look at the Treasury's website or for an international view look at the IPSAS website. The Treasury's website has a search engine and typing in 'financial statements' gives a number of different papers on the same theme, which it updates and deletes quite rapidly.

1.3 Accounting standards

There are a number of internationally accepted guardians of accounting standards.

- **The Accounting Standards Board:** 'The role of the Accounting Standards Board (ASB) is to issue accounting standards. It is recognised for that purpose under the Companies Act 1985. ... The ASB also collaborates with accounting standard-setters from other countries and the International Accounting Standards Board (IASB) both in order to influence the development of international standards and in order to ensure that its standards are developed with due regard to international developments.'

  Accounting standards developed by the ASB are contained in 'Financial Reporting Standards' (FRSs) and 'Statements of Standard Accounting Practice' (SSAPs). There are currently in the region of 30 FRSs and 12 SSAPs that organisations are expected to comply with in law in their published accounts.

- **International Accounting Standards Board (IASB):** 'Our mission is to develop, in the public interest, a single set of high quality, understandable and international financial reporting standards (IFRSs) for general purpose financial statements.'

  There are currently eight IFRSs and 41 international accounting standards (IASs) that organisations are expected to comply with in their published accounts.

  The accounting bodies report that the public sector is increasingly moving towards similar reporting standards as the private sector and the UK public sector has set 2008 to 2011 as the timetable to adopt IFRS.

- **General Accepted Accounting Principles:** If the IASB is responsible for developing brand-new accounting standards then Generally Accepted Accountancy Practice (GAAP) is the way in which a number of countries tend to adopt the standard, or at least interpret it, and fit it into their individual country's accounting standards. Each country has its own GAAP, but on the whole there aren't many differences between countries. UK GAAP is, effectively, the technical manual for the accounting bodies.

- **Institute for Public Sector Accounting Standards (IPSAS):** 'Compliance with the IPSAS standards guarantees that the financial reporting of public bodies conveys what is termed a true and fair view of the financial situation. IPSAS take account of the characteristic features of the public sector. Although the IPSAS are based on the IAS standards for private companies, they were adapted to the requirements of the public sector. The IPSAS are laid down by the International Federation of Accountants (IFAC), a private federation. They therefore have no legally binding force. The elaboration of the standards was, however, promoted and financed in the majority by the International Monetary Fund and the World Bank, of which Switzerland is a member.'

So, with all these wise and worldly bodies looking after the standards of our accounts, you would think the way financial data is put together into financial information would be standard. Not so! Take the example of depreciation.

The standardisation of depreciation

There are at least two very different ways in which depreciation can be calculated and, within reason, organisations are able to choose their own method and their own interpretation of key factors within that method.

So, if you want to buy a new file-server costing £100,000, the financial reporting standard (FRS) 15 covers the principles of accounting for tangible fixed assets. This 101-page guideline discusses as many variants as you can imagine on how an accountant can work out how much such an asset may have cost, yet doesn't set clear guidelines on the length of the period over which it should be depreciated. And neither should it. The point is that finance and accountancy is not a science. It's an art and the only answer you can guarantee you will get from an accountant is 'It depends'!

At this stage you need to remember the following:

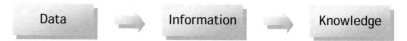

Have you identified financial data or financial information? It's actually a bit of both. Internally financial data is the raw data going into your accounting system. When using external 'information' it's really 'data' until you do something with it.

1.4   Validating financial data

If the adage of 'Garbage-in Garbage-out' is true, you should be looking to quality assure at both ends of the analysis process.

The internal auditor

Although the following definition of an internal auditor gives them a wider brief than you're looking at in this guide, internal auditors have traditionally been associated with the validation of internal financial information. Here's a quote taken from HM Treasury.

In essence, internal auditors help their organisations to manage risks. They keep senior-level executives up to date on key questions such as whether risks have been identified and how well they are being managed. They deal with issues that are fundamentally important to modern organisations. They look beyond the narrow focus of financial statements and financial risks to consider wider issues such as the organisation's reputation, its impact on the environment and the way it treats its employees.

For information on the role of the internal audit in the public sector, see Jones and Pendlebury's book *Public Sector Accounting*.

The authority matrix

Most organisations have some sort of formal or informal 'authority matrix' relating to what decisions can be made and by whom inside the organisation. This matrix is often not given the thought it deserves. In difficult times authority often resides in too few individuals, thus creating bottlenecks and discontent. When times are more optimistic, these are relaxed and then spending may get out of control.

Activity

Activity 1.4a	30 minutes

Review the financial authority levels in your organisation. Note the impact of this on the validity of the financial data in your organisation.

Note what these levels tell you about the approach to empowerment in your organisation.

Validating the financial process

A financial process is the same as any other process inside your organisation. Process-mapping will identify where possible errors or problems could occur in the system. For example, the financial system may expect that invoices are signed off by a number of senior managers before being passed on to the finance department for processing. This may result in invoices taking a long time before they are entered into the financial ledger and the costs of a project may therefore be understated.

 The checklist 'Implementing business process re-engineering' will help you consider how to redesign your financial processes so that quality is assured.

Validating the output

When it comes to financial information sometimes reasonableness seems to go out of the window. Financial figures should rarely be unexpected as long as they are:

- timely

- indicative

- relevant.

You'll look at the use of ratios as indicators in Topic 2 of this section.

The external auditor

Published information has the benefit of an independent audit. Despite the headline news of the collapse of major companies, this process is still relevant and, mostly, reliable. However, it only ensures that certain rules have been followed and certain standards adhered to. It does not ensure that the information produced by the company is in a comparable format to others or check whether or not the rules have been followed in one of the many differing and allowable ways. You should also remember that the auditors know the standards and conventions discussed earlier but they still rely on the business knowledge of the senior management of the company to set these in context.

It's interesting to look at who audits the auditors. There are two bodies:

 ■ **The Auditing Practices Board (APB):** This was established in 2002 and is part of the Financial Reporting Council. It is committed to leading the development of auditing practice in the UK and the Republic of Ireland in order to:

- establish high standards of auditing

- meet the developing needs of users of financial information

- ensure public confidence in the auditing process.

International Standards on Auditing (ISAs) for the UK and Ireland contain basic principles and essential procedures and apply to all audits of financial statements for periods since December 2004.

 ■ **IFAC (International Federation of Accountants):** 'We have long recognized that a fundamental way to protect the public interest is to develop, promote, and enforce internationally recognized standards as a means of ensuring the credibility of information upon which investors and other stakeholders depend.' IFAC's boards set the following standards:

- international standards on auditing, assurance engagements and related services

- international standards on quality control

- international code of ethics

- international education standards

- international public-sector accounting standards.

Roles and responsibilities

Generally, there are a number of people inside your organisation responsible for translating your financial data into information. The table below shows the roles and responsibilities of those involved in the purely financial part of the process.

Role	Responsibility
Book-keeper	Every business, no matter how large or small, is required by law to 'keep books'. This involves the recording of the financial transactions of a business, whether manually into ledgers or by entering everything on to a computer. The book-keeper then provides a business with accurate figures that enable it to know exactly how well it's doing.
Management accountant	Financial accountants (see below) traditionally focus on audit, tax and reporting on past performance, whereas management accountants look forward. They work at the heart of the business, evaluating and interpreting financial information so that they can make the strategic decisions that will shape an organisation's future. CIMA chartered management accountants are qualified to engage in a wide variety of activities: ■ advising managers about the financial implications of project management ■ explaining the financial consequences of management decisions, and suggesting actions ■ making strategic decisions and formulating business strategies to create wealth and shareholder value ■ monitoring spending and financial control ■ managing risk and business assurance ■ cost determination and financial control ■ evaluating existing financial information systems and suggesting improvements

SR 30

SR 31

Role	Responsibility
	■ conducting internal business audits and preparing periodic financial statements for managers ■ explaining the impact of the competitive landscape.
SR 32 Financial accountant	A financial accountant is responsible for the control of the financial management of a business, as well as advising and being involved in the strategic direction and administration of that business. Accountants extract and interpret information from the financial records for a wide range of interested parties throughout that organisation — shareholders, potential investors, bankers, employees, trade creditors and government departments. They're responsible for controlling the working capital of a business, ensuring debtors, creditors and stocks are maintained at an acceptable level, taking day-to-day decisions, giving advice to the board of directors (very often the financial accountant is a director of the company) and advising on capital investment. They're also responsible for the preparation of: ■ regular management accounts ■ budgets ■ reports on variance between actual performance and budget performance (any may have to recommend any remedial action) ■ interpretation of financial information — advising on trends.
SR 33 Treasurer	Treasury in a company is key in determining the financial strategy and financial policy, advising on what businesses to invest in, organising the appropriate funding and controlling the risk in the organisation. Depending on the risk environment, treasury will create an appropriate capital structure of debt and equity in order to fund the business, getting the optimum balance between cost and risk. This translates into the need to ensure that at all times the company has the liquidity and cash to meet its obligations as they fall due, taking in funding from equity or debt capital markets activities, bank borrowings, through to day-to-day cash management and investment.

Role	Responsibility
	Treasury is responsible for the identification of risks associated with this activity and for controlling risks that could erode financial strength, using mitigation and hedging techniques and encouraging a culture of sound financial practice.
	Treasury management is all about handling the banking requirements, the funding for the business and managing financial risk. It therefore incorporates raising and managing money, currency, commodity and interest-rate risk management and dealing, and in some organisations the related areas of insurance, pensions, property and taxation.
Public sector accountants	CIPFA's members work, often at the most senior levels, in public service bodies, in the national audit agencies and major accountancy firms. Their areas of expertise are the following: ■ leadership and strategic management ■ strategic and operational financial management ■ financial and performance reporting ■ governance, ethics and values ■ audit and accountability ■ partnerships and stakeholder relationships ■ change, risk and project management ■ procurement and contract management.

SR 34

You can see from the above, all the bodies are fighting for the same ground — to be perceived as the forward-looking business adviser rather than the traditional, grey-suited accountant.

Again, you need to look at this as a process and see how you can ensure this process has the best chance of providing you with timely, indicative and relevant information.

Financial information and knowledge management systems

Looking at the roles in the table above, many of them sound like they are taking on general leadership and management roles. So how do they differ from other functional managers inside your organisation?

SR 35

Perhaps the main difference lies in the accounting policies contained in FRS18 that govern the way an accountant thinks about an organisation. Before FRS18 (2000) one of the over-riding accounting concepts was 'prudence', which basically says that anything bad that can happen *will* happen so take it into account, and if there's anything good that may happen ignore it or think prudently. But now FRS18 refers to:

- true and fair view
- going concern
- accruals
- realisation.

Realisation, the fourth point above, is a similar concept to prudence, but with a little less doom and gloom.

Nevertheless, compared with other pieces of information in an organisation's knowledge management system, it's still safe to say that the accountant's view is likely to be more prudent than information from other sources. As a strategic leader, it's up to you to weigh up all the information on your organisation's knowledge bank and make decisions within the risk framework acceptable inside your organisation.

1.5   Organisational culture and financial control

The role of culture and the approach to financial control is an interesting area and one that has become more interesting to academics since the Enron collapse. However, most of the articles and comment seem to focus on the negative aspect of reducing control and pushing the accountancy profession back to 'prudence'. Contrast that with the view of other functions within an organisation and they may state that the financial controls imposed on them are restrictive and inhibit the development of the organisation.

There are often polarised views on financial control inside an organisation and it may simply be that different sub-cultures thrive within different functions and it's a leader's job to manage these. For example, accountants have to follow the accounting *rules*, whereas an operations department may be more used to dealing with things on an *ad hoc* basis. This could result in conflicting viewpoints on financial information as the accountant is more interested in whether they comply with standards whereas the Operations Manager is interested in how it can help solve a current problem.

Activity

Activity 1.5a		30 minutes
Look at the model 'Handy's four types of organisation culture' and identify a stereotypical culture for three functional roles (one being finance).		

Role	Culture	Areas of conflict in financial control
Function 1 Finance		

Function 2 Sales and Marketing		
Function 3 Operations		

If you were the general manager how could you bring these together to improve the financial management in your organisation?

Another cultural issue, one that's more prevalent in the public sector, is the end of year 'dash for cash' or need to 'spend the remaining budget'. The world of the accountant falls into discrete 12-month periods and the world ends at the financial year-end and starts afresh the very next day. This can have a huge behavioural impact inside an organisation. If you work in this type of organisation you'll know the negative impact it can have on the efficient use of financial resources in an organisation.

Supporting resources

Books

1   Atrill, P., and McLaney, E., 2007, *Management Accounting for Decision Makers,* FT Prentice Hall — although aimed at students of management accounting, it does set the subject within a management framework, with some good visuals and practice exercises.

2   Leech, C., *Financial Control* (Unit 5007), 2006, revised by Rowlings, R., 2008, Pathways series, Chartered Management

Institute — to check your underpinning knowledge before going on to Level 7.

3   Rice, A., 2007, *Accounts Demystified: the Astonishingly Simple Guide to Accounting*, Prentice Hall — a good introduction based more on words than numbers and taking away any fear for those looking at finance for the first time.

4   Fitzgerald, R., 2002, *Business Finance for Managers: An Essential Guide to Planning, Control and Decision Making*, Kogan Page — a comprehensive textbook covering both management discussion and the figures.

5   Bean, J., and Hussey, L., 1997, *Finance for Non-Financial Public Sector Managers*, HB Publications — a basic text using public sector terminology.

6   Jones, R., and Pendlebury, M., 2000, *Public Sector Accounting*, Prentice Hall — relates many of the issues in management and financial accounting to the public sector, including the role of the audit.

7   Ernst and Young, 2008, *International GAAP 2008: Generally Accepted Accounting Practices Under International Financial Reporting Standards* — for reference.

Articles

8   O'Reilly-Allen, M., and McMullen, D., 2002, 'Internal Control Reporting and Users' Perceptions of Financial Statement Reliability', *American Business Review*, January, pp. 100–7 — a statistical study of different ways of changing users' perception but without strong conclusions. **P+**

9   Eccles, T., and Holt, A., 2005, 'Financial Statements and Corporate Accounts: The Conceptual Framework', *Property Management*, Vol 23, No 5, pp. 374–87 — aimed at professional surveyors to increase their understanding of financial statements and covering many of the topics in this section.

10 Penno, M.C., 2008, 'Rules and Accounting: Vagueness in Conceptual Frameworks', *Accounting Horizons*, Vol 22, No 3, pp. 339–51 — a quantitative analysis on how people find accounting rules too vague, and also looks at what 'vague' actually means. **P+**

11 Reider, R., 2007, 'Financial Audits: Taking an Operational View', *Journal of Corporate Accounting and Finance*, May/June, pp. 19–25 — a look at how financial processes link into some of the operational processes in organisations. **P+**

12 Wolnizer, P.W., 1978, 'Independence in Auditing: An Incomplete Notion', *Abacus*, June, Vol 14, Issue 1, pp. 31–52 — based on an ongoing discussion in the US and Canada considering an auditing body as intermediary between the company and the external auditors. **P+**

Checklists

13 Internal audit. **P+**

14 Handling information avoiding overload. **P+**

15 Knowledge management. **P+**

16 Carrying out an information audit. **P+**

17 Implementing business process re-engineering. **P+**

Thinkers

18 Ikujiro Nonaka: Knowledge creation. **P+**

Models

19 Handy's four types of organisation culture. **P+**

Weblinks

20 www.keynote.co.uk

21 www.hm-treasury.gov.uk/ — www.hm-treasury.gov.uk/ psr_index.htm takes you to a section 'public spending and reporting', which has some interesting information.

22 www.ipsas.org/

23 www.frc.org.uk/asb/about/

24 www.iasb.org/Home.htm

25 www.cipfa.org.uk/pt/ifrs/

26 www.ipsas.org/en/ipsas_standards.htm

27 www.iia.org.uk/en/

28 www.frc.org.uk/apb/index.cfm

29 www.ifac.org

30 www.book-keepers.org/

31 www2.cimaglobal.com/cps/rde/xchg/SID-0A82C289-B4A47C06/live/root.xsl/25835.htm

32 www.ifa.org.uk/role.asp

33 www.treasurers.org/treasury

34 www.cipfa.org.uk/members/expertise.cfm

35 www.frc.org.uk/images/uploaded/documents/FRS%20181.pdf

36 www.pwc.com/extweb/pwcpublications.nsf/docid/C2A82DF2 F68D262F802569A1004F6835

Topic 2:   Analytical tools and techniques

Introduction

This topic turns to the processing and use of financial data and introduces the tools and techniques of financial analysis and interpretation.

There are many tools and techniques used for financial analysis, and many of these are ratios of financial information. Using a ratio combines information and can relate parts of the business together — often giving a deeper insight into what's going on. This topic introduces the stakeholders who will be interested in your financial information, considers the different ratios used to analyse an organisation, and looks at which ratios are more appropriate to which stakeholders. Finally, an interpretation of financial ratios is explained in order to better understand the position of an organisation.

2.1   The value of financial analysis

In the introduction to this guide we said that there was no such thing as finance — and this is where our meaning will become apparent. A financial analysis will not answer all your questions. But what it *will* do is raise intelligent questions and point you in the direction of others in your organisation who should know the answers. And if they don't, you need to know why they're not aware of the financial impact of their decisions.

Poor managers are often 'anti-accountants' because they hear accountants asking difficult questions. But it's important not to shoot the messenger as he or she is only trying to resolve issues raised through financial analysis. The better organisation and the better manager would actually have informed the accountants beforehand that there may be issues in the business that will reveal themselves in the financial figures from analysis.

Stakeholders and financial analysis

The Chartered Institute of Management's checklist 'Stakeholder analysis and management' identifies 'primary stakeholders' as any of the following:

- customers
- suppliers
- employees — managers with financial responsibility and accountants
- shareholders or investors
- your bank.

'Secondary stakeholders' can be the following:

- competitors
- consumer groups
- government — central or local government bodies
- the media
- pressure groups
- trade unions
- community groups.

In this guide you'll consider all the primary stakeholders as well as your competitors and government (especially with regard to taxation). If you work in the public sector you should also include consumer groups, or more simply 'the public'. You should also include external and internal auditors.

The difficulty for organisations and their senior management is that these stakeholders are all interested in different aspects of your financial performance and, in some cases, their requirements are actually contradictory. This is shown in the table below.

Stakeholder	Interests	Could conflict with
Shareholders	Share value Market capitalisation Rapid growth High gearing High retained profit Dividends	Banks Employees Customers Public
Bank	Cashflow Liquidity Interest cover Low gearing Steady growth Forced sale value Fixed assets for secured loans	Shareholders Managers
Employees	Job security Higher pay levels	Shareholders The public
Customers	Value for money Extended credit terms Business continuation	Shareholders Bank Accountants Employees
Suppliers	Cashflow Minimum credit terms Best price	Shareholders Bank Accountants

Stakeholder	Interests	Could conflict with
Competitors	Comparative gross margins Comparative net profit Comparative sales	
Government	Taxable profit Accuracy Audit Window dressing (making the published accounts look better than they would do at any other time of the year, e.g. by paying your suppliers more quickly than you might normally do) Fraud	Accountants
The public	Value for money Lower pay level Lower taxes	Employees Government
Your accountants	Prudence (or realisation) Accuracy Accounting standards Accounting principles	Everybody
You and your managers	In smaller companies the emphasis is on cashflow In medium-sized businesses and in departments of larger business the emphasis is on sales, cost and profit. In larger companies the emphasis is on the balance sheet and shareholder value. In the public sector the emphasis is on costs and best value.	Any of the above

Some of the terms in the table above are explained in the checklist 'Accounting ratios'. For a more detailed review of how to calculate financial ratios use Walsh's book *Key Management Ratios*.

The difficulty for you as a manager is that what one person sees as good management another person may see as poor management. Take the example of something as simple as creditor days or accounts payable. If this figure is high, some see this as good because you're keeping cash in the business, while others see this as poor management and a sign of your organisation being in financial difficulty.

2.2 Tools and techniques

There are a number of tools and techniques used in financial management and the table below indicates which stakeholders may use them and where this guide will help you understand what they are used for.

Tool/technique	Primary stakeholders	Explanation
Profitability ratios	Shareholders Customers Managers	This section
Liquidity ratios	Bank Suppliers	This section
Asset utilisation	Bank Shareholders	This section
Shareholder ratios	Shareholders Accountants	This section
Variance analysis	Managers	Section 2
Key financial indicators	Managers	Section 2
Investment appraisal	Accountants Managers	Section 3

As you can see, there are a number of different financial ratios and you'll start to look at the more popular ones next. The actual mathematical formulae for these are not set out here as you'll be concentrating on the different interpretations with reference to the stakeholder analysis introduced above. For a full explanation of all the formulae refer to the two resources suggested here.

Profitability ratios

First, here are six ratios used to determine profitability.

Ratio	Possible interpretations
Return on capital employed (ROCE)	This gives an indication of how well an organisation has used the money that has been invested in it. In theory this should be different to the ROI and ROE described below. The 'capital employed' should include all investments — both from shareholders and banks. (Many books don't make this distinction and use ROCE, ROI and ROE interchangeably.)
	In summary, ROCE looks at how much profit has been made compared with how much capital has been put into the organisation.
	For this ratio you should use operating profit as the indicator of profit as this is the profit you've

Ratio	Possible interpretations
	made before paying investors — i.e. before paying interest to the bank or dividends to the shareholders.
	For the capital employed figure you should then use all the money you've been given for investment — shareholders' funds plus bank loans.
	Ideally, this figure should at least exceed maximum gross interest rates. If not, as managers, you should move all the capital into high interest accounts and make more money that way.
	Organisations with high fixed assets (manufacturing companies) would expect to see lower ROCE than service organisations.
	This ratio needs to be monitored quarterly in most organisations and also when major changes in fixed assets or investment have happened.
Return on investment (ROI)	For all intents and purposes this is the same measure as the Return on equity that shareholders refer to. It lets the long-term investors — shareholders and venture capitalists — look at the return they're making on their investment and decide whether they would make a better return if they invested elsewhere.
	For this ratio you should use profit after interest as the indicator of profit as this is the profit you've made after paying the bank but before paying dividends to the shareholders.
	For the capital employed figure you would then use just the shareholders' funds.
	Low ROI doesn't mean that you won't get investment from shareholders. But it may mean that you'll only attract risk-averse shareholders or investment shareholders, which will mean you have to compensate them by paying higher dividends.
	This ratio needs to be monitored quarterly in most organisations and also when major changes in fixed assets or investment have happened.
Return on sales (ROS)	This is the potential profit you have to either reinvest in the business or pay out in dividends. It's also the 'bottom line' profitability that can be compared with the performance of your competitors.
Gross margin	Gross margin is said to give an indication of price and direct costs relative to your competitors. Many customers look at your accounts in this way. But use this figure with caution as an external benchmark because different companies treat direct and indirect costs in different ways.

Ratio	Possible interpretations
	Internally, this is an excellent measure and changes in it suggest either that you should make: ■ a change in price — talk to your sales team ■ a change in costs — talk to your production team ■ a change in product mix — talk to your marketing team. This ratio can be appropriate to the public sector if you're providing direct services such as building and works. For the purpose of assessing efficiency you should consider the total budget allowance as income and look at the direct costs as a percentage of this.
Expense ratios	This is another good internal measure in relation to sales. How much are you spending on the overheads or indirect costs? Most organisations will have a manager responsible for different aspects of the overheads and it's their responsibility to provide you with information that may effect the balance between their costs and the activity of the organisation. A growing organisation would initially expect to see economies of scale and therefore see expenses reducing as a percentage of income. However, rapid long-term growth will usually lead to the company having to invest in additional overheads (or fixed costs) and this will have a negative impact on this ratio in the short term. An organisation that restructures its costs between direct (variable) and indirect (fixed) will also see changes in this ratio. Good managers will have predicted these in their forecasts and they should not come as a surprise to the accountants for the organisation. This ratio is appropriate to the public sector. For the purpose of assessing the controls, you should consider the total budget allowance as income and look at the expenses as a percentage of this.
Interest burden or interest cover	If you have loans or overdrafts in the business they are going to cost you. The banks look at this as a key measure of your ability to continue to service the loan. If they see your profits falling significantly in relation to interest they are likely to want to renegotiate their loan terms with you. You need to understand your relationship with the bank to understand how close they will allow those figures to become. The economic climate will also impact on this figure because this changes the bank's attitude to risk.

Liquidity ratios

There are two liquidity ratios that are commonly used.

Ratio	Possible interpretations
Current ratio	This ratio is said to give banks and suppliers an indication of your ability to repay short-term borrowings and pay your suppliers. It's said to give the 'best case scenario' and shows how much cash or potential cash you have in your current assets and how much you might have to pay out in the near future.
	Although this ratio is used extensively by people who only have access to the published accounts, it should be used with caution and in combination with the stock, debtor and creditor ratios below.
	Banks often quote a 2:1 ratio as a minimum requirement and yet some service industries would automatically fail this test. The financial world is a different place now compared with what it was in the days of heavy manufacturing industries.
Quick ratio or acid test	This ratio is also said to give banks and suppliers an indication of your ability to repay short-term borrowings and pay your suppliers. However, it's said to give the 'worst case scenario' and shows how much cash or potential cash you have in your near liquid current assets (debtors and in the bank) and how much you might have to pay out in the near future.
	Again, this ratio is used extensively by people who only have access to the published accounts and should be used with caution and in combination with the debtor and creditor ratios below.
	Banks often quote a 1:1 ratio as a minimum requirement. But some retail industries would automatically fail this test as they don't have debtors and yet their cashflow is likely to be healthy in the short term.

Asset-utilisation ratios

There are four commonly used ratios relating to asset utilisation.

Ratio	Possible interpretations
Fixed asset utilisation	This ratio attempts to look at how hard you are working the fixed assets in your organisation. It probably really only has a significant meaning in heavily automated manufacturing organisations.
	Major changes in this could suggest new capital expenditure. Minor changes could suggest your machines are experiencing some idle time. However, this needs to be looked at alongside the stock calculation below as busy machines could result in stock piling rather than increased sales.

Ratio	Possible interpretations
Stock turnover/ days	Stock turnover or stock days gives an indication of how efficiently you are using your stock.
	However, you need to treat this with caution. In organisations with lots of stock the valuation of that stock — raw materials, work in progress and finished goods — can be complex. This complexity makes it an area of focus for the external auditors at the year end. The year-end accounts may be a reliable figure but can you say the same on a month-by-month basis? If not, and stock is an important aspect of your business, this may indicate that you need to invest in better stock-control software.
Debtor days	This is a measure most organisations pay attention to in both the private or public sector. In the public sector it may be more difficult to measure on a daily basis as many of the requests for payment, such as taxes, are on an annual, bi-annual or quarterly basis. As such, they need special systems to ensure monies are collected on a timely basis but in a manner that doesn't cause public resentment.
	In the private sector this figure is critical as non-collection of money owed is responsible for many company failures. Most good financial systems will have a sales ledger that can produce this figure by individual account so that actions can be taken as needed.
	Suppliers and customers alike will look at your statutory accounts to calculate the credit you allow your customers. Suppliers, like banks, will see a high figure as poor management that will impact on your ability to pay them. Customers will use this figure as a negotiation tool when trying to maximise their credit terms with you.
	In the annual accounts the 'dash for cash' often means that the debtors' figure is at its lowest for the whole year as a disproportionate amount of time is spent collecting money due to 'window dressing' of the published accounts.
Creditor days	This ratio is relevant in all sectors. In the public sector government has made the timely payment of suppliers one of its key performance indicators (KPIs), and has even introduced legislation to encourage companies to pay each other on time.
	In the private sector some accountants think it's a good technique to delay payment to creditors for as long as possible. But suppliers are increasingly wise to this and will stop supplies if this happens.
	In the published accounts extended creditor days

Ratio	Possible interpretations
	can be seen by potential investors — especially the banks — as a sign of poor management. This is because they see this as asking the creditors to take the strain for your inability to manage the cash. Banks are less likely to lend to organisations that have borrowed too much from their creditors.

Shareholder ratios

There are a total of seven ratios that are of interest to shareholders.

Ratio	Possible interpretations
Return on equity (ROE)	This is virtually the same measure as the Return on investment referred to in the profitability ratios. It lets the long-term investors (shareholders and venture capitalists) look at the return they are making on their investment and at whether they would make a better return if they invested elsewhere.
	Sometimes for this ratio people use profit after interest *and tax* as the indicator of profit as this is the profit left for potential reinvestment or dividends.
Growth	The return for shareholders comes from the growth in share price. This comes in part from the growth in the business.
	Shareholders are especially interested in the balance sheet growth of the shareholders' funds but will also be interested in the growth in sales and whether this has been reflected in a similar growth in profit.
Gearing	This indicates the balance between funding from shareholders (equity) and funding from lending institutions (loans). Highly geared organisations have a relatively high amount of loans in relation to equity. These organisations are considered to be much more risky especially by the lending institutions. Unfortunately this is in direct contrast with how it's viewed by shareholders who have invested in a company with high growth potential. There's more consideration of this in Development Guide 7007 *Financial planning*, but as a rough guide here, banks will never lend if the gearing is higher than 1:1 (for every pound put in by shareholders they would put in a pound) and they rarely get anywhere near this because of the way they view the 'worth of the business'.
Earnings per share	This is a measure based on how much profit could be shared out between the shareholders. It would then be up to the shareholders at the annual

Ratio	Possible interpretations
(EPS)	general meeting to decide how much of this should actually be paid out in dividend and how much to reinvest in the business.
Price earnings ratio (PE ratio)	This is a ratio relevant to the investor in relation to other investments in quoted companies and is really beyond the remit of this guide. However, if you read the *Financial Times* you'll see this figure quoted along with the share price. It's the market value of the share in relation to the earnings per share (EPS) and shows, at current profit levels, how long it would take to get all your money back. Ironically, a high PE ratio suggests a rapidly growing company as the Stock Exchange has priced it highly in relation to its current profit.
Dividend cover	This is similar to the interest burden or cover looked at by the banks. It simply looks at how much profit has been made in relation to the dividend paid and how easy it is for the organisation to 'cover' the payment of that dividend.
Dividend yield	Like the PE ratio, this is of more interest to the investor on the Stock Exchange and simply looks at how much dividend has been earned in relation to the price they have to pay for the shares. This is balanced with the possible growth in the market price of the share and the investors' attitude to risk.

Activity

Activity 2.2a   **1½ hours**

Find out what ratios are produced in your organisation. How do they compare with the lists above? Are there any that are missing that you think would be valuable and should be introduced? Make notes below.

Supporting resources

Books

1   Rice, A., 2007, *Accounts Demystified — The Astonishingly Simple Guide to Accounting*, Prentice Hall — a good introduction based more on words than numbers and taking away any fear for those looking at finance for the first time.

2   Walsh, C., 2008, *Key Management Ratios*, FT Prentice Hall — a surprisingly good read with internationally comparative ratios.

Articles

3   Eccles, T., and Holt, A., 2005, 'Financial statements and corporate accounts: the conceptual framework', *Property Management*, Vol 23, No 5, pp. 374–87 — aimed at professional surveyors to increase their understanding of financial statements and covering many of the topics in this section.

4   Penno, M.C., 2008, 'Rules and accounting: vagueness in conceptual frameworks', *Accounting Horizons*, Vol 22, No 3, pp. 339–51 — a quantitative analysis on how people find accounting rules vague, and also looking at what 'vague' actually means. **P+**

Checklists

5   Stakeholder analysis and management. **P+**

6   Making rational decisions. **P+**

7   Internal audit. **P+**

8   Reading a profit and loss statement. **P+**

9   Reading a balance sheet. **P+**

10 Shareholder value analysis. **P+**

11 Accounting ratios. **P+**

12 Five routes to greater profitability. **P+**

Weblinks

13 www.netmba.com — sets out the formulae for ratios.

14 www.tutor2u.net — as above.

Topic 3: Conducting comparative analysis of financial data

Introduction

This topic introduces comparative financial analysis. You can compare data using many criteria, such as across time, departments, products, customers, markets and companies. However, a key point to note is that comparing apples and pears will only confuse and certainly not gain you insight, knowledge or commercial advantage. You therefore need to be cautious in how, what and when you compare. You'll look in particular at the value of comparing past and present performance and comparing performance against that of competitors.

Comparing past and present performance can be meaningful, but the longer the timespan the less effective or accurate this may be. Comparing across years depends upon the stability of the organisation — whether its strategy, operations, pricing, cost structure, products and customers have remained reasonably constant. Comparing your performance against competitors' performance can be even more fraught, as you may not know the relevant changes made in these organisations over the time period of analysis.

Nevertheless, comparisons are very useful, and if used with caution they can bring new insight and knowledge about your own performance as well as that of your competitors.

In this topic you'll look at a case study of a medium-sized business in the service sector.

3.1 Case study

Scenario

New Fire Ltd

New Fire Ltd designs and project-manages furnace and large boiler refurbishments. The company employs 71 people full time and was founded in 1967 by John Gilford. It has sold itself on two main claims: Its 'cradle to grave' service and its skill base. Design is seen by the current directors as the real value-added service.

All employees are currently employed on a full-time basis. All wages are paid on a basic plus overtime basis. The direct wages of the business include designers, refurbishment engineers and project managers. The indirect wages include the rest of the management team and the administrative staff. There are currently 71 employees.

Commercial issues

The last financial year has been a challenge. The clients have less money to spend but the work still needs to be done. Because many clients have been with the business for years the directors have allowed them considerable discounts to help them through this difficult period. It's hoped that the clients will respond in kind when the economy improves.

The business experiences extreme seasonal fluctuations. The major refurbishments take place in the summer months when factories have traditionally had their holidays.

Credit control has also been an issue. It's not common practice to receive payment until the job is finished and the industry is not known for prompt payment. Payment terms are 30 days from the approval date of the project. This creates an unknown factor, as projects are often completed weeks before they've been given formal approval.

Completed projects have traditionally been treated as work In progress and invoices are raised once approval has been received. Once invoices have been raised, the average time it takes the customers to pay is between 30 and 60 days.

The valuation of work in progress is the most difficult part of the accounting process and its accuracy (other than at the year end date) is subject to question.

The type of work undertaken is shown below:

Furnace refurbishment (in steel works)	40%
Ships	25%
Factory work	15%
Hospitals	10%
Other	10%

The furnace refurbishment and factory work take place mostly in the summer and Christmas breaks. Eighty per cent of the refurbishment work relies on a few major clients. These clients have furnaces throughout the EU that need at least one major refurbishment every year. These equate to ten major projects every year with six starting in the summer and four in the winter. Other clients account for five projects spread over the year.

The hospital and factory work is very much based on traditional plumbing work but on a large scale. The company adds value by looking after the whole project.

The ship work requires the project team to work away from home. The work has to be done at the quickest speed possible in order to reduce the time the ship will be in dock.

In order to keep the gangs busy during off-peak times they have taken on less specialised work, such as general cleaning and repainting of large installations. This work is obtained through general advertising in the trade press and is not closely monitored.

Project management issues

The project managers each seek to have the best designers and engineers on their jobs. This can make training an issue as less experienced staff need to shadow more experienced staff. This is seen as a drain on the project managers' overworked resources.

The ship work is the most complex to manage due to the time factor. Design work can't start until the designer has been aboard ship and the most experienced engineers have to be used to meet the tight deadlines. As such, the company tries to limit this type of work to off-peak times when there are more people to chose from.

Design issues

Design basically covers everything that's not related to standard project management. The designers do the following:

- plan the projects
- identify the materials to be used
- produce the tender
- hand over to the project manager.

There are only a few competitors in this industry, so the success rate with tenders has been relatively high. New Fire usually wins 50 per cent of the tenders it submits, which means that designers can spend up to 50 per cent of their time on tenders that are not accepted.

Financial analysis

Below is a financial ratio analysis prepared by the company's accountant.

	This year	Last year	Previous year
Return on investment	23.60%	55.39%	65.53%
Return on sales	4.64%	10.89%	13.13%
Gross margin	28.13%	35.40%	36.83%
Interest burden	3.78%	1.39%	1.22%
Current ratio	1.57	1.35	1.29
Quick ratio	1.24	1.07	0.94
Stock days	33.36	35.45	40.68
Debtor days	89	89	69
Creditor days	45	58	52
Growth in net worth	15.20%	9.24%	
Growth in sales	12.36%	11.11%	
Growth in profit	(52%)	(14%)	

Activity

Activity 3.1a	30 minutes

Look closely at the ratios listed above, and bearing in mind the background of the company, comment on what the ratios confirm or reveal about New Fire's situation.

Activity

Activity 3.1b	30 minutes

Now reflect on the ratios used in your own organisation. Note where you can match the changing activities of your organisation over this period to the information reflected in the ratios.

3.2   Comparisons with competitors

Looking at your own financial performance can be very insular. Every organisation needs some comparator to start with in order to understand whether they've done well or not. Financial comparison should, where possible, be included in an organisation's benchmarking exercises.

You'll now look at a competitor of New Fire Ltd.

Burnace and Flast is a much bigger company than New Fire and operates just in the furnace sector of the market. It designs and builds furnaces as well as refurbishing and maintaining them. Design and build doesn't have to cope with the seasonal issues faced by the refurbishment market. This accounts for 80 per cent of the company's work, while refurbishment and maintenance accounts for just 20 per cent. Due to the large-scale capital nature of its core market it can demand pre-payment on large projects.

Burnace and Flast employs world-class project managers and has a technically competent sales team. However, 80 per cent of the direct work is sub-contracted. New Fire is one of its sub-contractors.

Although based in the UK Burnace and Flast has an international reputation, which has protected it from some of the commercial and seasonal issues in the UK.

The current-year comparative financial analysis is shown below.

	New Fire	Burnace & Flast
Return on investment	23.60%	25.48%
Return on sales	4.64%	5.48%
Gross margin	28.13%	25.28%
Interest burden	3.78%	3.95%
Current ratio	1.57	4.01
Quick ratio	1.24	3.03
Stock days	33.36	26.34
Debtor days	89	61
Creditor days	45	50
Growth in net worth	15.20%	8%
Growth in sales	12.36%	5%
Growth in profit	(52%)	10%

Activity

Activity 3.2a   30 minutes

Compare the ratios of the two companies and comment on what this tells you about their relative performance.

Activity

Activity 3.2b   1 hour

Try to get hold of a set of the most recent published accounts of one of your competitors. If it's a limited company these should be available from Companies House.

What insight does the information and figures give you into what may be happening in the marketplace?

What recommendations could you make to your organisation based on this financial benchmarking exercise?

Supporting resources

Books

1   Rice, A., 2007, *Accounts Demystified – The Astonishingly Simple Guide to Accounting*, Prentice Hall – a good introduction based more on words than numbers and taking away any fear for those looking at finance for the first time.

2   Walsh, C., 2008, *Key Management Ratios*, FT Prentice Hall – a surprisingly good read with internationally comparative ratios.

3   Fitzgerald, R., 2002, *Business Finance for Managers: An Essential Guide to Planning Control and Decision Making*, Kogan Page – a comprehensive textbook covering both management discussion and the figures.

Checklists

4   Reading a profit and loss statement. **P+**

5   Reading a balance sheet. **P+**

6   Shareholder value analysis. **P+**

7   Accounting ratios. **P+**

8   A programme for benchmarking. **P+**

Topic 4: The pitfalls of financial analysis

Introduction

This final topic introduces some of the major points to consider when analysing financial statements and ratios. You shouldn't be discouraged by its complexity from using such financial information, but do use it with caution.

You'll look at the limitations in financial systems and how to remove them by redesigning your financial system to be more of an information provider than simply a control provider. You'll look at the weaknesses in comparative ratio analysis and see how you can build strengths into any ratio analysis by using industry norms.

4.1 Redesigning the financial system

When looking at reviewing financial data you need to consider the financial processes. In the diagram below (produced as part of a conference paper in May 2007), Gabriel F. Sékaly from the Institute of Public Administration of Canada looked at the key competences of the new chief finance officer (CFO).

Traditionally, the way to ensure reliability in financial data had been to emphasise the controls and concentrate on centralised transaction processing. Sékaly, however, suggests that the better way to achieve this end is by inverting the triangle. The processing can be reduced by allowing data entry at point of responsibility and the control function can be reduced by process redesign.

Inverting the triangle will have a two-fold benefit for organisations:

- a reduction in data-entry errors

- increased time for management accountants to work on decision support and risk management in order to benefit managers and the organisation. Management accountants will effectively become internal consultants providing the financial information to support management decisions, adding the appropriate voice of caution and doing 'what-if' analyses to look at how risky the decisions may be.

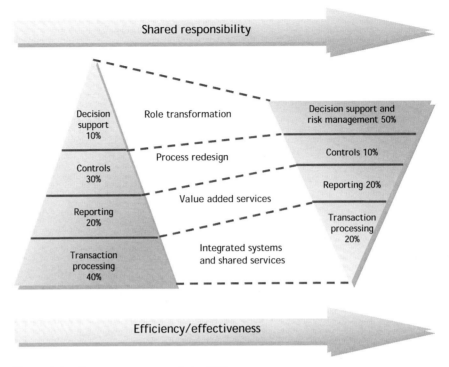

Figure 4.1a: Key competences of the CFO

4.2   The limitations of comparative ratios

In this section you've already seen how many internal and external bodies there are that are responsible for setting standards and auditing financial inputs and outputs. This has a major impact in the following areas of comparison.

	Different accounting policies	Ratios effected
Profit and loss	Differing depreciation policies result in differing cost of depreciation in either the direct or indirect costs	Return on capital employed Return on sales
Balance sheet	Differing depreciation policies result in differing net book values of fixed assets Stock valuation Debtor provisions Revaluations	Return on capital employed Fixed asset utilisation Stock turnover Debtor days

Depreciation

A simplistic example of this relating to depreciation would be as follows.

Two companies invest in a new computer system costing £100,000. One company may have a policy to depreciate this over five years, while the other may depreciate it over four years. In the third year this could mean the following.

	Company A	Company B
Cost	100,000	100,000
Depreciation year one	20,000	25,000
Depreciation year two	20,000	25,000
Depreciation year three	20,000	25,000
Book value at end of year three	40,000	25,000

The costs in company A in the third year would be 20,000 compared with 25,000 in company B and the balance sheet value of the fixed asset would be 40,000 in company A and 25,000 in company B. This would make company A appear more profitable and worth more.

Both these options would be acceptable under the guidelines of the financial reporting standards. Although the information on depreciation policy has to be disclosed in the published accounts, the complexity of this information on all fixed assets can make true competitor comparisons difficult. The recommended website gives information on the impact of depreciation and the different methods of calculation.

Creative accounting

Some organisations also apply creative accounting to show better financial performance. These can be small adjustments such as bad debt provisions and changing collection and payment values at the year end. These simply massage the year end figures.

Or they can be major manipulations or complications:

- revaluations of fixed assets such as buildings
- sale and leaseback of fixed assets such as cars
- goodwill
- intangible assets.

These can have a dramatic effect on the ratios calculated. They all have strict and complex guidelines in the financial reporting standards and, for the non-financial specialist, there can seem to be a fine line between window dressing and fraud. If this interests you, there are some tips on spotting fraud in the checklist 'Spotting fraud'.

Using business acumen to interpret ratios

Ratios are simply that — ratios: they relate one figure to another. In your own organisation they should help you and other managers to recognise the results of your management decisions on the financial performance. When doing a comparative analysis you may not have the same insight. In the case study used earlier, the analysis raised more questions than it answered. The background to New Fire Ltd allowed you to make some educated guesses about the business and why the ratios showed the trends they had. But the competitor's background was less detailed and the comparative analysis was more difficult, with a lot of guesswork needed.

Timeliness of information

In a traditional ratio analysis timeliness is one of the biggest limitations. If you're looking at a set of published accounts in November 2008 they probably relate to a year end dated December 2007 and contain data relating to the two periods starting January 2005 and ending December 2007. Some of the data is therefore up to four years old. Several things could have happened over this time, including the following.

Inflation	The stated value of such things as sales may seem smaller than they are if they relate to a period four years ago. For example, £1 million pounds four years ago could be the equivalent of £1.2 million today if there had been 5 per cent inflation each year.
Technology	In a high technology business the balance of the fixed (non-current) assets on the balance sheet could vary quite a lot over a four-year period.
Accounting policies and practices	Again using the high technology business, it's not unprecedented for the accounting treatment of these fast-moving fixed assets to have changed. If you take computers, they used to last up to four years and be depreciated over that period. Now many companies depreciate them over just two or three years.
Changes in interest rates	A company four years ago may have had a high interest burden and may be considered as risky. But if this was not due to a large loan but to high interest rates, and interest rates go down, the risk also looks much less.

Another aspect of timeliness is the year end of the accounts. Two competitors in the same market may have different year end dates. In many organisations this may not matter but in a seasonal business it could. If a holiday company had a financial year end in December and is compared with one with a year end in March, the amount of money received as deposits could appear to be radically different and this would impact on the balance sheet. If one company was heavily involved in skiing holidays this could also impact on the comparative analysis.

4.3 Industry norms

To overcome some of the limitations discussed, it's possible to compare against 'industry norms'. These are average figures for similar companies within an industry sector. These companies should be a good comparison as they operate within the same bounds and typically access the same type of suppliers and customers. Industry data can also smooth out differences due to industry trends, which all organisations operating in that sector will have been exposed to, to some extent. This smoothing out makes comparisons more relevant. Furthermore, standard interpretation of many ratios can be incorrect when applied within certain sectors. For example, a web-based company may have few real assets and so asset ratios could be seen as weak against normal standards, but strong against an industry norm.

You can find the industry norms for some ratios from organisations who provide databases of financial information (see the website in Supporting resources for one of them).

Activity

Activity 4.3a	30+ minutes

If you're interested in looking further into this, use the suggested website and search for your own industry norms (or use a different database if you have access to one).

Supporting resources

Books

1   Atrill, P., and McLaney, E., 2007, *Management Accounting for Decision Makers,* FT Prentice Hall — although aimed at students of management accounting, it does set the subject within a management framework with some good visuals and practice exercises.

2   Leech, C., *Financial Control*, 5007, Pathways series, Chartered Management Institute — to check your underpinning knowledge before going onto Level 7.

3   Rice, A., 2007, *Accounts Demystified — The Astonishingly Simple Guide to Accounting*, Prentice Hall — a good introduction based more on words than numbers and taking away any fear for those looking at finance for the first time.

4   Fitzgerald, R., 2002, *Business Finance for Managers: An Essential Guide to Planning Control and Decision Making,* Kogan Page — a comprehensive text book covering both management discussion and the figures.

Articles

5   Brewer, P., 2008, 'Redefining management accounting — the four pillars of our profession', *Strategic Finance*, March, pp. 27—34 — an interesting paper looking at how management accounting should broaden its horizon, with a number of checklists to assess how well you do in these areas. **P+**

6   Kaminski, K.A., Sterling Wetzel, T., and Guan, L., 1990, 'Can financial ratios detect fraudulent financial reporting?', *Managerial Auditing Journal*, pp. 15—28 — a comparison of accounts provided by companies that had been accused of fraudulent reporting and those that had not.

7   Ezzamel, M., Hoskin, K., and Macve, R., 1990 'Managing it all by numbers: A review of Johnson and Kaplan's "Relevance Lost"', *Accounting and Business Research*, Vol 20, No 78, pp. 153—66 — an international review of accounting history

and how they relate to 'managerialism' to see if the groundbreaking paper is still relevant. **P+**

Checklists

8   Shareholder value analysis. **P+**

9   A programme for benchmarking. **P+**

10 Implementing best value. **P+**

11 Internal audit. **P+**

12 Handling information avoiding overload. **P+**

13 Spotting fraud. **P+**

Weblinks

14 www.accountingweb.co.uk/cgi-bin/item.cgi?id=38170

15 www.dnb.com/

Section summary

In this section you've looked at analysing financial data, covering the following:

Topic 1: Assessing the validity of financial data

- what is financial data? (1.1)
- the reliability of financial data (1.2)
- accounting standards (1.3)
- validating financial data (1.4)
- organisational culture and financial control (1.5)

Topic 2: Analytical tools and techniques

- value of financial analysis (2.1)
- tools and techniques (2.2)

Topic 3: Conducting a comparative analysis of financial data

- New Fire Ltd case study (3.1)
- comparisons with competitors (3.2)

Topic 4: The pitfalls of financial analysis

- redesigning your financial system (4.1)
- the limitations of comparative ratios (4.2)
- industry norms (4.3)

Activity

Section summary activity	3 hours

Produce a report for your organisation suggesting improvements you could see might be possible in the structure of your finance department and its relationship with the rest of the organisation covering:

- the book-keeping and processing of financial information
- the controls and authority levels for financial decisions
- the format of financial information in the management accounts
- the format of financial information in the published accounts
- the financial information managers currently use to make decisions
- the financial information managers could use to make decisions.

Section 2 Budgets and organisational objectives

Introduction

In this section you'll look at a simplified approach to financial analysis using key financial indicators (KFIs) and linking these to the budgeting process. A more simplified analysis combined with visual representations of performance improves a manager's ability to communicate using financial information and to better communicate with the accountants.

You'll look at how budgets can be produced taking into account financial constraints, achievement of targets, legal requirements and accounting conventions. You'll then see how to analyse the budget outcomes against organisation objectives and identify alternatives.

Note that in this guide the main focus is on budgets and other short-term financial tools. Longer-term financial planning is the subject of Development Guide 7007 *Financial planning*.

In this section the focus is on revenue budgets, while capital budgets are considered in Section 3.

Learning outcomes

This section covers the following learning outcome:

7003.2   Be able to assess budgets based on financial data to support organisational objectives

Section mind map

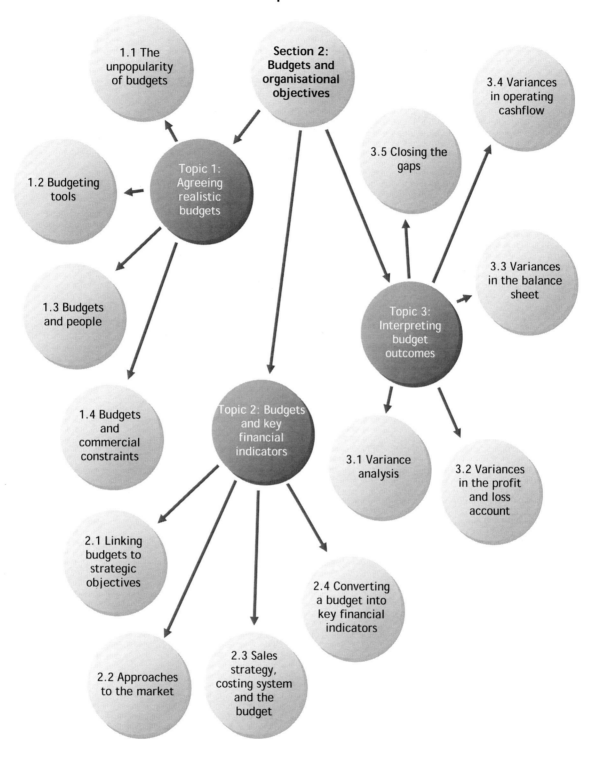

Topic 1:   Agreeing realistic budgets

Introduction

There are many systems used inside organisations to try to predict, control and monitor performance — strategic plans, business plans, balanced scorecards, key performance indicators and budgets. While budgets do generate organisational debate (often not very positive), they don't attract the same interest and debate as other systems.

In this topic you'll look at what budgeting is and its relevance today, budget tools, how budgeting impacts on organisational behaviour and who should be involved in the different steps of budgeting, and what commercial constraints need to be built into budgets.

Ekholm and Wallin researched company's attitudes to budgets to address the question 'Is the annual budget really dead?'. The main findings seem to suggest not.

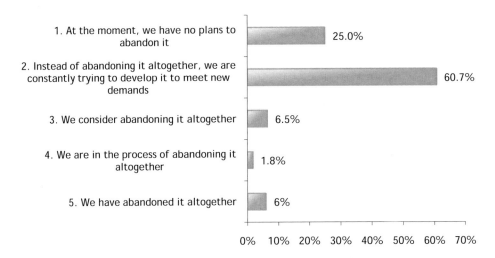

So, although budgeting may not be the most popular performance management tool in an organisation, it would seem you'll be working with it for some time to come.

1.1   The unpopularity of budgets

Budgeting is at the heart of the way organisations measure what they want to achieve. It's a key tool in planning and integrating activities, allocating funds and achieving strategic aims. Organisations are increasingly involving other staff, as well as accountants and finance directors, in drawing up a budget.

Why is budgeting not as popular as other performance measures? It's a fact that many managers consider finance and accounting a bit of a black art and this feeling can be exploited by accountants and consultants and have a negative impact on behaviour inside an organisation. It's often difficult for managers to see what they want to achieve in the figures produced in a traditional budget.

Criticisms of budgets include the following:

Unsuitable in the knowledge age	Budgets are often about process, and process finds it difficult to capture true knowledge. In psychological terms, process is about 'sensing' and knowledge is about 'intuition'.
Rigid thinking	You often only look at the financial implications the budgeting process asks you to look at. Unusual impacts may be ignored.
Incremental thinking	It's very difficult not to be constrained by history and many budget guidelines often say things like 'There will be a wage increase in the budget of 3 per cent.' Budgets often end up being 'last year plus'.
Short-termism	Budgets are often annual, which is quite short term in itself. The nearer you get to the end of the budget year the shorter your time-frame becomes.
Ritualised	In some organisations the ritual is 'If I ask for £100,000 they will cut it back and I will get the £80,000 I wanted' so all budgets in the first draft are inflated.
Constraint	An opportunity during the budget year may be missed because it wasn't foreseen at the time of the budget and the number one priority is to achieve the budget at all costs.
Time-consuming	Some budgeting processes go through many iterations and take so long they're not finished until well into the year in which they are supposed to be implemented.

But all of the above could be said to be criticisms of the process and not the tool.

 According to Atrill and McLaney, the more positive aspects of budgets are as follows.

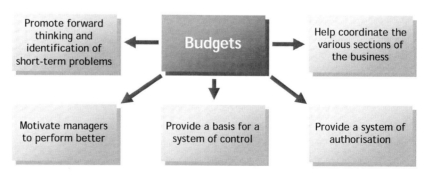

Figure 1.1a: Positive aspects of budgeting
Source: Atrill and McLaney (2007)

Another interesting dynamic of the budgeting process is the games people play around it in some organisations. A study carried out by Christopher Bart into the games product managers played has identified the following in six out of eight firms interviewed.

Language used		
slush fund	cookie jar	war chest
hedge	hip/back pocket	contingency
flexibility	kitty or secret reserve	
Budget games played		
Understating volume estimates	Overstated expenses:	
Undeclared/understated price increases	■ advertising	
Undeclared/understated cost reduction programs	■ consumer promotions	
	■ trade-related	
	■ market research	
	Undeclared line extensions	

See the recommended article by Bart for more details on this.

1.2   Budgeting tools

This review of some common budgeting tools is restricted initially to the financial issues before you consider the role of these financial issues in achieving strategic objectives.

- **Zero-based budgeting (ZBB)**: This is an approach to budgeting that starts from the premise that no costs or activities should be factored into the plans for the forthcoming period, just because they figured in the costs or activities for the current or previous periods. Rather, everything that is to be included in the budget, must be considered and justified. ZBB goes as far as to prompt the question 'Do we need the activity or service in the first place'.

- **Incremental budgeting**: This is the traditional method of preparing a budget forecast. It involves taking the previous year's budget and adding incremental amounts for the new budget period to meet the new situation, rather than starting from nothing as with ZBB. An incremental budget treats existing programmes and departments as already approved, subject only to increases or decreases in the financial resources allocated. Incremental budgets often lead to simplistic extrapolation and limit managers in terms of their conceptual thinking.

- **Rolling forecasts**: As the name suggests, these are not fixed in the same way as an annual budget might be. They may follow a similar format but are updated monthly or quarterly, both by changing the figures in the original budget or by 'adding on' extra months to the end. The advantage of this is that, unlike the annual budget, management attention is still looking at least 12 months ahead at all times — not just during the annual budgeting process. However, the constant updating may force the organisation towards the incremental approach to budgeting rather than taking a more strategic view.

Activity

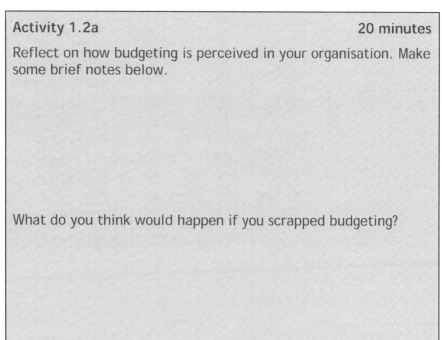

Activity 1.2a   20 minutes

Reflect on how budgeting is perceived in your organisation. Make some brief notes below.

What do you think would happen if you scrapped budgeting?

1.3   Budgets and people

You first need to identify who is, and who should be, involved in the budgeting process and at what stages. To do this you need to understand your organisation's approach to budgeting — top down versus bottom up.

Top-down budgets start by allocating budgets across the top tier of the hierarchy. Each manager then divides that budget between the layers below and so on. The assumption behind this approach is that the more senior managers are able to look strategically and prioritise between the different budgets.

Bottom-up budgets are similar in concept to zero-based budgets. The basic tasks are budgeted and added up into departments and so on, up and up the chain.

According to Atrill and McLaney, there are four possible impacts of budgets on performance:

■ Their existence tends to improve performance.

■ Demanding yet achievable budgets are more motivating than less demanding targets.

■ Unrealistically demanding budgets demotivate.

■ Participation in target setting improves motivation and performance

This suggests that, like other objectives, budgets need to appear to be SMART. In financial analysis a slightly different version of the SMART acronym is used.

Specific	Budgets need to be built on specific assumptions. For example, it's not specific just to say sales are going to increase by 5 per cent. You need to say why — will it be changes in price, volume, new markets, new products and so on.
Measurable	Finance is often seen as the measurable part of a plan but it needs to be part of a rounded set of measures. There are two sides to the financial measures: 1 Avoid 'analysis paralysis'. If budgeting systems are too complicated they will be ignored or populated with incorrect data. 2 If it's important, put a system in to measure it. We sometimes produce budgets in a way that we can't tell whether the budget has been achieved or not because there aren't any reports to give that information. So, if a measure is important, the financial system needs to be changed to support the monitoring of actual performance.
Agreed	This is where this version of SMART differs most. In line with Atrill and McLaney's four impacts of budgets, there's more likelihood of achieving budgets if you set demanding but achievable budgets and these are agreed with those responsible for achieving them.
Realistic	Realistic includes the concepts of achievable and relevant. Realistic isn't just in terms of the amount of the budget but also the nature of the budget — for example, taking into account external factors. The budget must also seem relevant in terms of the organisation and its overall goals and culture.
Timely	Time is very important to accountants. Timely in financial terms will relate to annual budgets, rolling budgets and the way these budgets are distributed over the budgeting period.

Activity

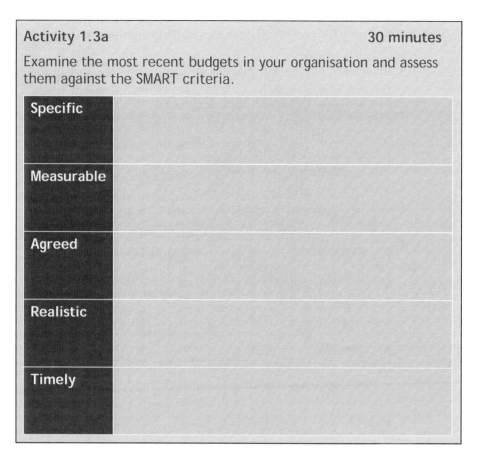

Who should be involved?

In order to identify who should be involved in the budgeting process in your organisation you need to understand the steps involved and then identify who would best be involved in each of these steps.

According to Atrill and McLaney, there should be nine steps in the budgeting process.

Step 1	Establish who will take responsibility.
	The nature of this task suggests this should be done by senior management.
Step 2	Communicate budget guidelines to relevant managers.
	This needs the involvement of senior management to ensure appropriate importance is given to the process. It also needs the involvement of the management accountants as they are the best people to coordinate the budgeting process and give expert advice on the budgeting guidelines.
Step 3	Identify the key or limiting factors.
	This is an interesting step as most managers at all levels will perceive this in a different way (you'll consider financial constraints later in this section).
	To ensure appropriate budget behaviour all budget holders should be involved in the discussions around this area.

Step 4	Prepare the budget for the area of the limiting factor.
	This is said to set the ceiling for all other activities. For example, if sales are the limiting factor, the sales forecast should be designed and agreed before the other departments. Identifying the limiting factor will stop the bad budgeting practice of going through many iterations of the process until one hangs together properly.
Step 5	Prepare draft budgets for all other areas.
	The other budget holders can only budget successfully when they know the activity level they are expected to support.
	Having said that, each budget holder will be trying to get the most beneficial budget possible and there will still be some lack of coordination between them.
	The budget holders will be the prime people involved at this stage. They may need the support of the internal accountants, but this time in their role as consultants rather than financial controllers.
Step 6	Review and coordinate budgets.
	Due to a lack of coordination there needs to be some element of professional expertise to see whether the area budgets add up to a coherent whole and have not created another limiting factor.
Step 7	Prepare the master budgets.
	These are likely to be in the format of the traditional financial statements, and the management accountants would normally produce them.
Step 8	Communicate the budgets to all interested parties
	It's important that senior management clearly communicates the final version of the budget. Ideally, the budgets should be clearly communicated across the whole organisation to avoid the feeling of secrecy and favouritism that the budgeting process can produce.
Step 9	Monitor performance against the budget.
	You'll look at this later in this section.

Activity

Activity 1.3b	30 minutes

Which of the above steps are covered in your budgeting process?

Who are the main people involved at each step? Make notes alongside the table if you wish.

Who has budget responsibility inside your organisation? Does this reflect the needs of the organisation and its desire to achieve the overall organisational budget? Make notes below.

1.4 Budgets and commercial constraints

The first thing to consider is what is likely to be included in a budget. If you exclude capital spend, budgets are likely to cover the following areas.

From the profit and loss account	From the balance sheet	From the cashflow
Sales	Stock	Short-term funding
Direct costs	Debtors	
Indirect costs	Creditors	

The table below shows what may create a financial constraint for each of these.

Budget item	Constraint on financial performance
Sales/ income	In the private sector the market and your products will put constraints on price and volume, which will impact on your gross profit.
	Price can be constrained by competition, perceived quality and required speed of delivery. It's also constrained by more long-term and strategic issues (these are looked at in more depth in Development Guide 7007 *Financial planning*).
	Volume can be constrained by the amount you're able, or prepared, to spend on marketing and selling your products or services.
	Local authority income can depend on what level of the organisation you look at and can include large, almost fixed items such as taxation, and smaller more variable items like fines and parking fees. The smaller items may react in a similar way to sales and have price and volume constraints. The first can be more predictable if set at policy level.
Direct costs	The interplay between direct costs and finance can relate to such costs as direct labour. This can again have price and volume constraints on the budget. How do your direct-labour levels compare with those of your competitors? How easy is it to attract appropriately qualified labour in your area — both geographical and industrial? If demand exceeds supply, you may have to increase wage levels — which will impact on your costs and gross profit.
	The other major constraint in this area will be the supply of materials. The price of materials will depend on your power in relation to your supplier (see Michael Porter, under 'Thinkers').
Indirect costs	There can be some significant constraints in the indirect costs. These are often referred to as the 'fixed costs' and tend to move up or down in major chunks rather than as a smooth line.
	Some fixed-cost elements are more limiting than others such as the costs related to the site or offices you occupy. It's a huge decision to decide whether you allow your operations to expand so far that you need to move to new premises. The reverse side of this is that if you have high fixed costs to cover, you may be forced to keep operations at a certain scale even if the market conditions make this a less favourable option.

SR 13

Budget item	Constraint on financial performance
Stock	Closely related to issues of sales volume and supply, stock is often one of the key indicators of your efficiency in managing the working capital. As a result, stock control measures and 'just in time' philosophies have become popular. In manufacturing, output capacity of your machinery stock can also affect availability. In the short term this physical constraint can be reduced by spending on sub-contract manufacturing if available. In the long term you may need to consider whether the funds are available and the risk is acceptable for additional capital investment.
Debtors	Money in the hands of your customers instead of in your bank can result in a severe financial constraint on your operations. Budgets need to go beyond simply making the sale, they also need to consider what payment terms they're prepared to offer and how much they're prepared to spend on credit control to achieve these.
Creditors	Creditors are often seen as the flex in the working capital cycle. But again the power relationship with your suppliers may turn off this source of 'cheap' cash.
Short-term funding	In this section you're only considering short-term funding as investors are not enthusiastic about funding increases in working capital, and incremental growth often has to be achieved from these short-term funding sources.

The following are some of the issues relating to the constraints listed above. These are taken from Michael C. Thomsett's book The *Little Black Book of Budgets and Forecasts*, which discusses ten particular constraints. Here they are in brief.

- Losing sight of real objectives:
  - Budgeting procedures are too complex.
  - Too many revisions are carried out.
  - Lack of review procedures.
  - Over-reaction to variances.
  - Used as a tool to improve business performance.
- Budgeting above 100 per cent of previous year:
  - Producing expenses as 'last year plus'.
  - Historical information is only one source of information.
  - Last year's overspend is not an indication that a bigger budget is needed.

- Always look for greater efficiency.
- Getting rich on paper
  - Putting in figures that just look good but are like a fantasy novel.
  - This may be to satisfy banks or head office.
  - Eventually you'll lose credibility if you never make your targets.
- Accepting arbitrary changes:
  - Don't accept other people's assumptions if you don't believe or understand them.
  - Don't accept across the board changes in assumptions.
  - When dealing with a manager stick to the facts and avoid ego confrontations.
- Believing that bigger is always better:
  - Why should sales always increase every year?
  - Remember the busy fool syndrome.
  - Remember businesses have life cycles and ups and downs.
  - Sometimes you have to invest now to realise later.
- Responding to 'explanation pressure':
  - Problems can be solved only when you know what they are.
  - Always revisit your assumptions when giving explanations.
  - Recommend solutions rather than placing blame.
- Depending heavily on statistics:
  - Don't try to manipulate the facts.
  - Don't hide answers under numerical comparisons.
  - Don't try to go back to previous years to explain current problems.
- Keeping inaccurate budgets in effect:
  - If budgets need changing, change them now and not at the next revision date.
- Accepting responsibility without authority:
  - If you don't have authority, don't come on too heavy with your recommendations.
  - Talk to other departments if your recommendations involve them.
- Failing to recommend
  - Budgets often become too passive and 'soft' recommendations are not acted on.

Supporting resources

Books

1 Atrill, P., and McLaney, E., 2007, *Management Accounting for Decision Makers,* FT Prentice Hall — although aimed at students of management accounting it does set the subject within a management framework, with some good visuals and practice exercises.

2 Thomsett, M.C., 1988, *The Little Black Book of Budgets and Forecasts,* AMACOM — now out of print but the ten constraints still apply.

Articles

3 Ekholm, B., and Wallin, J., 2000, 'Is the Annual Budget Really Dead?', *The European Accounting Review*, Vol 9, Issue 4, pp. 519—39.

4 Bart, C.K., 1988, 'Budgeting Gamesmanship', *The Academy of Management*, Vol II, No 4, pp. 285—94. **P+**

5 Bruggeman, W., and Van der Stede, W., 1993, 'Fitting Management Control Systems to Competitive Advantage', *British Journal of Management*, Vol 4, pp. 205—18. **P+**

Checklists

6 Setting SMART objectives. **P+**

7 Drawing up a budget. **P+**

8 Establishing a performance management system. **P+**

9 A programme for benchmarking. **P+**

Models

10 Zero-based budgeting. **P+**

11 Incremental budgeting. **P+**

Thinkers

12 Robert Kaplan and David Norton: The balanced scorecard. **P+**

13 Michael Porter: What is Strategy? **P+**

Topic 2: Budgets and key financial indicators

Introduction

This topic introduces the production of a budget and the use of key financial indicators to monitor progress against it. Production of a budget should involve all key stakeholders in integrating their knowledge about the projects and tasks to be achieved within the budget in order to best assure accuracy. However, budgets are sometimes imposed by accountants or managers who are trying simply to limit costs rather than truly understand operational activities and the relevant constraints.

You'll look at the linking of budgets to strategic objectives by considering the strategic planning process and the role of the budget. You'll then look at your approach to the market and the impact on the budget, while understanding how sales strategy and the costing system also impact on the budget. Finally you'll convert your budget into key financial indicators.

2.1 Linking budgets to strategic objectives

Budgets and plans should be set within the performance framework of your organisation, such as the balanced scorecard. An interesting article on where budgets fit into the strategic cycle can be found in Kaplan and Norton's article 'Mastering the management system' suggesting the budget should come after the performance framework has been put together not before. Whatever your approach, a budget serves two main purposes:

- It lets you plan what might happen.

- It lets you see if what you planned might happen did happen.

Budgets are a means to the end and not the end itself. But a budget badly prepared is not worth the effort you put into it. Budgeting encourages you to think ahead and coordinate different functions (sales, production, labour), and provides an instrument of control enabling you to manage by exception — that is, take action on what differs from expected rather than trying to control everything. This means finalising the budget should be more than an annual exercise, but instead should be part of the everyday management of the performance of the organisation.

Finance and the business plan

Finance is simply the numbers part of the plan and is no more or no less important than the rest of that plan. You should treat the plan as a whole thing so that the financial figures are a true numeric representation of the narrative contained within the plan. Not only must you look at internal issues but you must also be aware of the conditions external to the organisation. The further into the future you look, the less certain you become and the more uncertain your budgets are. (For background information on budgeting see the supporting resources.)

The financial plan is the final element that falls out of the whole strategic process. The figure below is taken from a public sector business-planning process and shows the many repetitions these financial stages should go through in order to get a budget that can gain commitment from everyone. Too often budgets are at the back of the strategic or business plan and the links between the narrative and the numbers can be hard to establish.

Figure 2.1a: A typical public-sector planning process

Again, in this section, you're only going to deal with the short-term element of the budgets these represent.

From the profit and loss account	From the balance sheet	From the cashflow
Sales	Stock	Short-term funding
Direct costs	Debtors	
Indirect costs	Creditors	

The elements of the budget with a longer-term impact are discussed in Section 3.

2.2 Approaches to the market

As mentioned in the previous topic, financial constraints can come from the perception of quality in relation to price. According to Kotler and Keller in their book *Marketing Management*, you have a choice of the following nine strategies when looking strategically at sales.

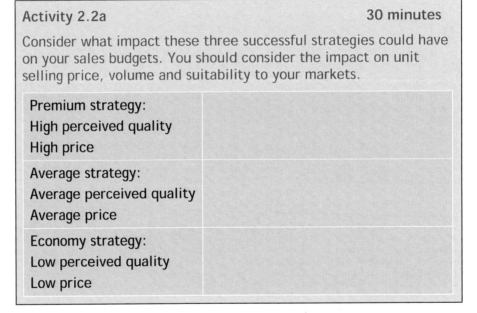

Figure 2.2a: Nine strategies for sales
Source: Kotler and Keller

Where you position your product will impact on the budgeted sales value. According to Kotler and Keller, strategies 1, 5 or 9 are potentially successful.

Activity

Activity 2.2a	30 minutes

Consider what impact these three successful strategies could have on your sales budgets. You should consider the impact on unit selling price, volume and suitability to your markets.

Premium strategy: High perceived quality High price	
Average strategy: Average perceived quality Average price	
Economy strategy: Low perceived quality Low price	

This concept is explored in more detail in Development Guide 7007 *Financial planning* but, for now, it is important to realise that the sales strategy is key to developing the cost structure within the organisation. A high price/high quality strategy will mean additional costs have to be invested in ensuring you deliver what the customer expects.

You now need to move on to discussing the cost structure within the budget.

2.3 Sales strategy, costing system and the budget

Here you're going to look at two significant items that will impact on the costs in the budget:

■ sales strategy

■ costing system.

Sales strategy

Decisions about sales strategy will affect the cost structure. Your sales strategy will affect direct costs as a quality product or service needs to have quality engineered into it — and that costs money. The figure below, taken from John Thompson's *Strategic Management*, shows the additional investment in cost that needs to be made in order to achieve the extra profit that a high-quality product or service can bring. But profit is never guaranteed and the additional investment in cost can therefore be risky.

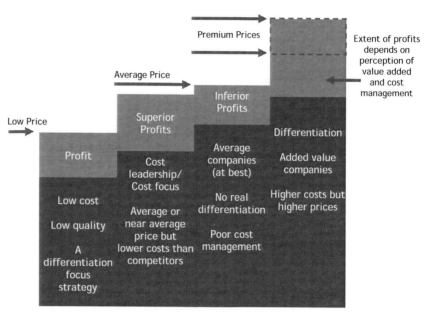

Figure 2.3a: The relationship of price, perception and profit
Source: John Thompson, Strategic Management

In the fourth bar of the graph (on the far right) the cost budgets could be geared up for a high-quality product or service and perform well against budget. However, sales may not meet the anticipated price or the volume is not possible at the set price. The budgets are now out of balance in the organisation, with one department looking at costs, thinking they are performing well, whilst another — sales — is under-performing against budget, and the organisation as a whole is under budget in terms of profit.

Costing system

Another strategic decision which impacts on costs is the costing system used in the organisation. Using a sophisticated costing system such as activity-based costing (ABC) impacts both on the cost structure of the organisation and the way budgets are distributed and used inside the organisation.

The figure below shows the result of a survey into why organisations choose to adopt ABC.

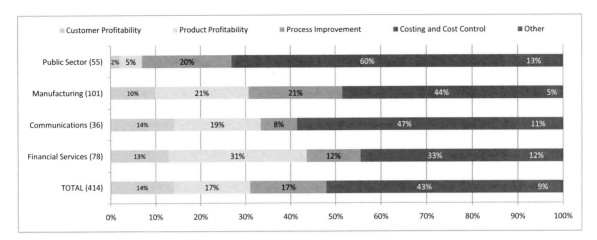

Figure 2.3b: Survey on ABC

 Costing and cost control (usually via budgets and variance analysis) are consistently the most important driver, especially in the public sector. A surprising factor was the use of the system for product profitability in the financial services sector. This could suggest that in this sector budgets are devolved along product lines. For more information on activity-based costing read Atrill and McLaney's book *Management Accounting for Decision Makers*.

2.4 Converting a budget into key financial indicators

Traditionally, budgets have been pages of fairly formalised financial information. Many managers find the task of absorbing that amount of figures difficult, which has an affect on their attitude towards the budget. As in the rest of management literature, it helps if you focus on what is key in the figures.

 At department level, key financial indicators (KFIs) can form part of an organisational performance measurement system such as Kaplan and Norton's balanced scorecard. Bill Snaith and Jane Walker in the book *Managing Tomorrow Today: Dynamic Financial Management* move away from the traditional budget format to focus on four aspects:

- Key — what's really important to a specific manager.

- Indicator — presented in a way that's indicative of performance within an organisational context rather than stated as an absolute value.

- Timeliness — it's better to give managers something quickly rather than something that is 100 per cent accurate (note that accuracy in management accounts differs between industries).

- Presentation — wherever possible, present these indicators in a visual format. An interested or intrigued manager will dig deeper into the figures when they spot a worsening trend in a graph.

In this guide you're not going to look at departmental financial indicators within the balanced scorecard as these could be so many and various depending on sector and department. Instead, you're going to focus on KFIs at company level since these can be fairly standard.

The first radical change of mindset when using KFIs is the calculation of ratios (or indicators). If you looked closely at the formulae for the ratios you'll know they are difficult to remember. So, to keep it simple, all KFIs can be stated as a percentage of your month's income — be it sales or budget allocation. This is because this is the line that should drive your activity and therefore your costs and working capital.

The table below shows how this works.

Gross profit %	Efficiency
	Gross profit is, in effect, the real income into the business. As a senior manager you have to manage four things:
	■ the income level — price
	■ the income level — volume
	■ the associated direct costs
	■ the product mix.
	How efficient your management of these is will be reflected in the gross profit percentage. Monitoring this will give you an indication of whether you have got the price right in the market, whether your product range is attractive and reflects a balanced portfolio approach, and whether you're managing the direct costs to their maximum productivity level (lean management).
Net profit %	Effectiveness
	Once you've budgeted your level of activity (sales volume) you need to construct an organisational infrastructure that will support this level of activity. What marketing efforts will be needed and how will this translate into marketing spend and the size of the marketing team? The same questions go for administrative support and other areas.
	These infrastructure items often involve taking on indirect or fixed costs, which can be difficult to get rid of if activity levels don't meet their budgeted level. Working effectively can therefore be a lot more difficult than just looking at efficiency.
Stock %	Traditionally, this has been said to represent the amount of stock you need to service your future sales. This will be determined by your understanding of 'just in time' management, manufacturing or supplier lead times, your service level agreement with customers on delivery times and so on.

	Often stock is incorrectly omitted in service industries. Long-term projects, such as consultancy, with fixed-period invoicing, can cause the net profit percentage to jump all over the place. This is often because there's a large amount of human capital tied up in work in progress that hasn't been reported correctly in the management accounts.
Debtors %	Debtors are simply money you've lent customers as part of the sales negotiation. In line with price, quality and volume terms this is an equally relevant part of the deal. Yet do all your customers pay on time? Probably not, yet they would be the first to shout if you decided to charge a different price than that agreed. Representing these as a percentage of sales just makes it easier to calculate. A figure of 100 per cent indicates that they are about one month old, while 150 per cent indicates 1½ months old and so on.
Creditors %	Creditors are simply money your suppliers have allowed you to borrow from them interest-free. This sounds like an attractive source of borrowing but this should only be done as part of the original negotiation and not by breaking those terms. Representing these as a percentage of sales just makes it easier to calculate. The figure does not translate easily into days but it does give a true comparison against the debtors' figure. If debtors' percentage is 100 per cent and creditors' percentage is 50 per cent you have twice as much money owing to you as you owe to your suppliers.

For many managers, graphs are an easier way to look at financial information and to quickly identify where that KFI is at variance with the expected. Graphs can be produced for all the KFIs listed above. In this topic we are just going to look at the profitability one, while in the next topic, after you have looked in more detail at variance analysis, you can then look at graphs relating to stock, debtors and creditors.

One possible graph to show your budgeted and actual performance of your profitability KFIs is shown below.

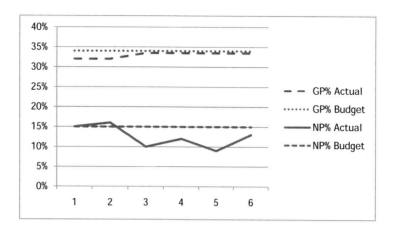

Figure 2.4a: Budgeted vs actual profitability percentages

This graph for a six-month period would suggest that the gross profitability of your organisation is pretty much on target. However, the net profit is a lot more variable and, after a good start to the period, has shown a significant decline. As gross profit seems all right then this would suggest there is something wrong in the relationship between the volume of activity and the indirect costs structure of the organisation. As the position is improving at the end of the period this suggest that management action has been taken to rectify this problem — possibly by reducing some of the indirect costs.

Activity

> ### Activity 2.4a   1 hour
>
> Plot your gross profit percentage and net profit percentage for the last six or twelve months against both the actual and budget figures. Do this on a separate sheet of paper.
>
> What do they reveal about your business and its management of its efficiency and effectiveness?

Supporting resources

Books

1   Atrill, P., and McLaney, E., 2007, *Management Accounting for Decision Makers,* FT Prentice Hall — although aimed at students of management accounting, it does set the subject within a management framework, with some good visuals and practice exercises.

2   Kotler, P., and Keller, K., 2008, *Marketing Management* Pearson Education — not specifically relevant for this guide but a useful cross-subject reference.

3   Thompson, J., 2001, *Strategic Management: Awareness and Change*, Thomson Learning — not specifically relevant for this guide but another useful cross-subject reference.

4   Snaith, W., and Walker, J., 2001, *Managing Tomorrow Today: Dynamic Financial Management*, FT Prentice Hall — the authors of this guide's own take on finance, linking dynamic indicators together to allow simple financial modelling.

Articles

5   Kaplan, R.S., and Norton, D.P., 2008, 'Mastering the management system', *Harvard Business Review*, Jan, pp. 62–77 **P+**

Checklists

6   Drawing up a budget. **P+**

7   Writing a business plan. **P+**

8   Implementing best value. **P+**

9   Implementing the balanced scorecard. **P+**

10 Setting SMART objectives. **P+**

11 Establishing a performance management system. **P+**

Thinkers

12 Robert Kaplan and David Norton: The balanced scorecard. **P+**

E-learning modules

13 Managing financial and non-financial resources. **P+**

Weblinks

14 'Activity-based costing: how ABC is used in the organization', September 2005 http://www.sas.com/offices/europe/switzerland/romandie/pdf/actualites/abm_survey_result.pdf

Topic 3: Interpreting budget outcomes

Introduction

This topic considers operating within a budget and the possible diversions that can occur. In particular, you'll review why actual performance varies from the budgeted performance, how to identify the cause of variance in profitability, working assets and in operating cashflow, and finally, and most importantly, how to close the gaps.

The topic introduces in-depth variance analysis that should help you get to the root cause of any difference between the budget and your actual performance. Again, finance is not about giving answers but about providing you with intelligent questions to ask.

A budget is only worth doing if you then do something with it. Some budgets are ignored, because they were imposed or because the organisation doesn't have sufficient controls, or maybe just because they were DUMB: Doubtful, Unquantifiable, Meaningless and Boring! Instead, budgets have to be designed well and agreed with those involved — and such budgets are the ones that are SMART.

 For background information on controlling a budget take a look at the checklist 'Controlling a budget'.

3.1 Variance analysis

There are five main reasons why actual costs vary from budgeted costs:

- incorrect budget assumptions

- timing differences

- changes in the cost of individual items — price variance

- changes in the number of items bought — volume variance

- human error.

Activity

Activity 3.1a	30 minutes
Give examples of when these may happen in your organisation	

Incorrect budget assumptions	
Timing	
Price or cost changes	
Volume changes	
Human error	

Before moving to close any gaps caused by variances, you need to be sure where the error is. Is it in the budget or in the actual performance?

To avoid some of the variances from either the budget being wrong or human error you should consider how committed people were to the budget in the first place. For more on this see Chong and Chong's article 'Budget Goal Commitment and Performance'.

3.2 Variances in the profit and loss account

Variances can also be caused in different parts of your budget. The three most common parts are in:

- sales
- direct costs
- indirect costs.

In the example that follows you're going to look at wages/salary cost variances — a cost that all business have and a good example to show the principle of variance analysis. To understand how these might impact on sales or other costs, you should look at J.R. Dyson's book *Accounting for Non-Accounting Students*.

Price variance may also be referred to as rate, budget or spending variances, while volume variances may be referred to as use or efficiency variances.

Variance analysis requires you to really understand what your labour should cost in the first place and how long each person should be spending on each task — a concept known as 'standard costing'. This is something that manufacturing is used to looking at but that is less common in the service and public sectors. This may be due to a lack of understanding of why it's done and the benefits it could bring. The biggest resistance is 'You can't do it in this industry as there's no such thing as a standard service.' This may be true but it can be used as an excuse for not holding the appropriate people responsible for their performance against budget.

Eleven steps to identifying a standard time in any industry are as follows:

1. Establish the standard task method.

2. Break down the task into activities.

3. Study the productive activities.

6. Rate the worker's performance.

8. Compute the average time.

9. Compute the normal time = (average time) x (rating factor).

10. Compute the standard time = (normal time) x (allowance factor).

11. Work out how many should be done.

This technique is used in organisations as non-standard as social work. It links closely to some of the techniques used for lean management and activity-based costing. It seeks to identify standard costs including direct and indirect costs.

The diagram below helps explains how you can understand the underlying root cause of the variance.

Calculation of direct labour variances

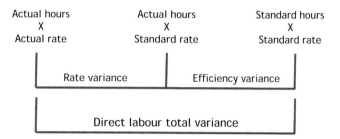

Figure 3.2a: Underlying root cause of variance
Source: Adapted from Dyson

The example explains the diagram:

A company makes cabinets and the deluxe model has the following labour requirements:

Direct labour per cabinet: 4 hours x £7 per hour = £28 per cabinet

During the current month it manufactures 1,200 cabinets, the same as its budget. The breakdown of financial information relating to labour costs is as follows:

Direct labour: Total hours: 4,750 hours

Total cost: £33,725

The following table is the variance between rate and efficiency.

	Actual hours x 4,750	Actual rate = £7.10	£33,725
Rate variance	Actual hours x 4,750	Standard rate £7.00	£33,250
		Unfavourable variance	**(£475)**
	Actual hours x 4,750	Standard rate £7.00	£33,250
Efficiency variance	Standard hours x 1,200 x 4 hours =4,800	Standard rate £7.00	£33,600
		Favourable variance	**£350**
		Total variance – unfavourable	**(£125)**

The real problem with this organisation is the cost of the labour hour, which could be due to poor management of overtime. The actual efficiency/productivity is higher than expected and the labour force should be commended for this.

Without the detailed variance analysis it's difficult to see how to tackle variances and get the budget back on track. It may even be, as is common in the public sector, that higher than expected wage increases have been given (over which the manager has little control). This would show that the budget now is wrong and the manager should be commended for the real efficiencies in their department and encouraged to look for more of these.

Activity

Activity 3.2a		30 minutes
Note down what could cause variances in your organisation.		
	Price/rate variance	Volume/efficiency variance
Income		
Who would be responsible for each of these?		
Direct costs — labour		
Who would be responsible for each of these?		
Direct costs — other		
Who would be responsible for each of these?		
Indirect costs		
Who would be responsible for each of these?		

3.3   Variances in the balance sheet

Again, you're only going to look at short-term variances in the working capital. You'll look at long-term variance in Section 3.

Variances in the working capital can mean the difference between survival and bankruptcy. The problem with stock, debtor and creditor variances is that they will also vary with sales. An adverse variance with regard to cash can be because of a positive variance in sales — because the more you sell, the more stock you have to buy, and yet the payment for these increased sales may take two or three months to be realised.

 Traditional ratio analysis and ways of looking at these working assets does not always reveal the true problems that may be building up for a business. For a traditional approach to managing working capital see the checklist: 'Managing working capital'.

An alternative way to look at these is in relation to sales.

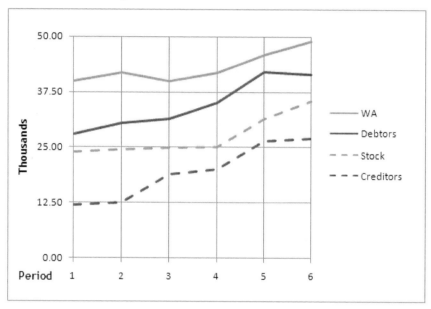

Figure 3.3a: Working assets graph (value)

This graph above shows the movements in stock, debtors and creditors, with the working asset line (WA) being the net impact of the three. If looked at independently, this looks bad. The value of stock and debtors has increased dramatically over the six-month period. The creditors have also increased but not enough to compensate for the money tied up in stock and debtors.

To understand whether these are badly managed, they need to be compared with sales activity. This is best done by restating them as a percentage of sales. This is discussed in Snaith and Walker's *Managing Tomorrow Today: Dynamic Financial Management* (2001).

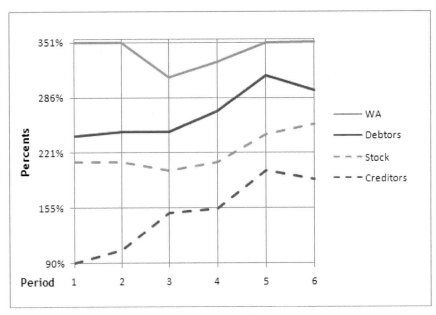

Figure 3.3b: Working assets graph (percentage)

How do you interpret the graph above? First, look at the debtors' line. At the beginning of the period they were 240 per cent of the sales for that month. This is the equivalent of 1 month (30 days) x 240 per cent = 72 days. In month 5 they rise to their highest level at 312 per cent. Again, this is the equivalent of 30 days x 312 per cent = 94 days. The debtors are way out of line.

What should the percentage graph look like? It should be a straight line. If a good debtors' figure as a percentage of a month's sales in this business is 240 per cent, they should stay at 240 per cent every month. If a business is growing, its debtors are going to go up and it will need more stock just to furnish these sales. If the management of this is out of control as well — revealed in the percentage figure — the business could be running out of control and out of cash.

Activity

Activity 3.3a	1 hour

Plot your debtors, creditors, stock (if you have it) and working assets for the past six or twelve months both as a value and a percentage of sales. Do this on a separate sheet of paper or in Excel.

What do they reveal about your business and its management of its operating cash?

3.4 Variances in operating cashflow

Variances in short-term cash can only come from two sources:

- not enough profit

- too much cash tied up in working assets.

Operational cashflow can be improved by either increasing profit or by reducing the working assets that you carry within the organisation. Increasing profit is clearly not easy in practice but is simple in theory — either increase your prices or volume or reduce your costs. Again, reducing your working assets is not easy in practice, and is done by better stock management, debtor recovery or increasing creditor days. But do note the effect this would have on supplier relationships before doing this.

3.5 Closing the gaps

Business is really quite simple. If there are gaps between your budgeted performance and your actual performance you need to work to close the gaps. There are actually only seven things you can do.

To close gaps in your net profit, the decisions you can make are as follows:

- Increase your prices.

- Increase your volume.

- Reduce your direct or variable costs.

- Reduce your indirect or fixed costs.

Any change can be related to one of these four categories.

There are only a few extra decisions you can make to improve working assets:

- Debtors can change.

- Stock can change.

- Creditors can change.

And, as pointed out above, managing net profit and managing working assets will impact on your operating cashflow.

So, in summary, there are two types of decisions to make:

- those affecting your contribution

- those affecting your stock, debtors and creditors.

SR   6, 7, 9

The following checklists are helpful here:

- Controlling costs

- Five routes to greater profitability

- Stock control.

Supporting resources

Books

1 Atrill, P., and McLaney, E., 2007, *Management Accounting for Decision Makers,* FT Prentice Hall — although aimed at students of management accounting, it does set the subject within a management framework, with some good visuals and practice exercises.

2 Dyson, J.R., 2007, *Accounting for Non-Accounting Students,* FT Prentice Hall — a detailed textbook that will fill in any missing gaps.

3 Snaith, W., and Walker, J., 2001, *Managing Tomorrow Today: Dynamic Financial Management,* FT Prentice Hall — the authors of this guide's own take on finance linking dynamic indicators together to allow simple financial modelling.

Articles

4 Chong, V.K., and Chong, K.M., 2002, 'Budget Goal Commitment and Performance', *Behavioral Research In Accounting,* Vol 14, pp. 65–86 — links the issues of budget, motivation and performance using quantitative analysis. **P+**

Checklists

5 Controlling a budget. **P+**

6 Controlling costs. **P+**

7 Five routes to greater profitability. **P+**

8 Managing working capital. **P+**

9 Stock control. **P+**

Section summary

This section has looked at the process and analysis of budgets and their variances. You've focused on the short term and dynamic elements of the budget and will look at major capital discussions in Section 3.

Topic 1: Agreeing realistic budgets

- the unpopularity of budgets (1.1)
- budget tools (1.2)
- budgets and people (1.3)
- budgets and commercial constraints (1.4)

Topic 2: Budgets and key financial indicators

- linking budgets to strategic objectives (2.1)
- approaches to the market (2.2)
- sales strategy, costing system and the budget (2.3)
- converting a budget into key financial indicators (2.4)

Topic 3: Interpreting budget outcomes

- variance analysis (3.1)
- variances in the profit and loss account (3.2)
- variances in the balance sheet (3.3)
- working in operating cashflow (3.4)
- closing the gaps (3.5)

Activity

Section summary activity	1 hour

Examine the way your organisation reviews performance against budgets.

- What information does it produce to help this?

- How does it approach variance analysis?

■ How are managers held accountable and responsible for their budget performance?

■ What steps are taken to re-forecast information in line with the actual performance against budget?

Section 3 Evaluating financial proposals

Introduction

In this section the focus is on capital budgets. In the last section you looked at revenue budgets and here you'll consider the whole aspect of incorporating both revenue and capital issues into a business proposal that's not part of the normal budgeting process.

You'll identify the criteria by which to judge proposals and evaluate the impact of the proposal on the strategic objectives of the organisation. You'll also analyse the viability of a proposal for expenditure, identify its strengths and weaknesses and give feedback on it.

Learning outcomes

This section covers the following learning outcome:

7003.3   Be able to evaluate financial proposals for expenditure submitted by others

Longer-term financial planning is the subject of Development Guide 7007 *Financial planning.*

Section mind map

There are three topics in this section as shown below. Check the subjects within each one and then continue with the areas you need to explore.

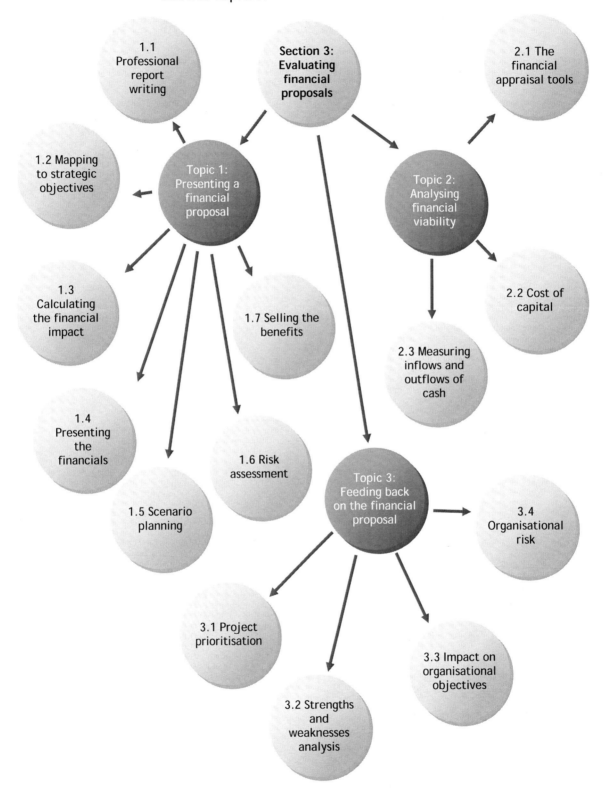

Topic 1: Presenting a financial proposal

Introduction

In this topic you'll consider how to put together a convincing proposal for financial expenditure. This brings together many skills you should have developed as a senior manager:

■ oral communication skills

■ business planning

■ budgeting

■ capital appraisal

■ analysing alternatives

■ assessing risk

■ written communication skills

■ writing an effective business case.

All these skills have to come together, while showing that you possess both commercial and financial acumen in a way that can convince both a board of directors and the 'prudent' financial specialists.

You also have to recognise that your proposal may be in competition with other proposals. An organisation doesn't have a limitless treasure trove of cash to give to every project. It is also a fine line between selling and over-selling your ideas, with risk and reward (personal and organisational) being the key selection criteria.

1.1 Professional report writing

Activity

Activity 1.1a   **30 minutes**

What current criteria are used in your organisation to assess proposals with a financial impact on your organisation?

The first criteria for evaluating a financial proposal is going to be the way you set it out, especially if it contains a lot of financial information. Many managers find page upon page of figures at best boring and at worst incomprehensible. So you need to ensure this part of your proposal is neither of these.

The checklist 'Effective business writing' is a good introduction into the writing style needed for any business proposal and the checklist 'Writing a business plan' will give a flavour of the specific content needed for a business plan.

For the public sector the BERR website offers the following as a template for a good business case:

- background

- scope

- objectives

- berr strategy

- options

- proposed solution

- benefits

- risks

- dependencies

- affordability

- analysis of costs and phasing of expenditure

- critical success factors

- procurement procedures (if applicable)

- additional information.

Finding out your own organisational template or using a best practice approach can only improve the professionalism of the business case. One of the trickiest aspects, and the area of most interest here, is how to incorporate the financial proposal. The two supporting resources suggested here give valuable guidance.

In addition to a written proposal, it's possible that you'll be asked to give a verbal presentation on your request. An effective business presentation should use objective language to persuade the audience that the information is accurate, deserving of consideration, relevant and important.

1.2   Mapping to strategic objectives

A good business case will show how your proposal will help your organisation achieve its objectives. A simple matrix should suffice, as shown below.

Organisation's strategic objectives	Impact of this proposal
Objective 1	Explanation
Objective 2	Explanation

1.3 Calculating the financial impact

Depending on the nature of the project you're proposing these could include:

- forecast profit and loss accounts
- forecast balance sheets
- cashflow forecasts
- payback analysis
- discounted cashflows
- ratio analysis
- key financial indicators.

SR 1, 3, 2

Some of these have already been discussed in detail in Topic 2. For additional information you could read Atrill and McLaney's *Management Accounting for Decision Makers* or Fitzgerald's *Business Finance for Managers*. For a background look at the profit and loss account and balance sheet you could refer to Rice's *Accounts Demystified*.

1.4 Presenting the financials

When doing a proposal with potentially complex financial information, it can be difficult to think of an interesting way in which to present it — especially when the people reading it may have different levels of knowledge, different approaches to analytical material and possibly different styles. Your proposal is likely to be read by a number of people all with different preferences.

For example, there are said to be four types of behaviour related to communication and that each type requires to be communicated with in a different way. The table below outlines each of the four types and suggests approaches for each type. You should find this quite interesting if you're not already familiar with it.

Dominant communication type	Communication approach
Goals/results oriented, loves challenge, impatient, task oriented, high achiever, workaholic, decisive, stubborn, blunt, innovative, tough/firm in relationships, control oriented, competitive	Be specific, clear and brief Stick to business Present the facts logically Ask specific questions (what?) Provide service choices Provide facts and figures

	Disagree with the facts not the person
	Refer to objectives and results
	Support and maintain
	Use discretion

Expressive communication type	Communication Approach
Dreamer, unrealistic goals, creative, needs approval and compliments, generalises, persuasive, outgoing, opinionated, fast decisions, excitable and enthusiastic, shows confidence	Plan interaction to support intuition
	Be stimulating
	Be sociable and casual
	Be fast moving
	Talk about people
	Talk about their goals
	Avoid extensive detail
	Ask for their opinions
	Provide ideas for implementation
	Provide testimonials
	Offer special incentives
	Recognise their accomplishments

Solid communication type	Communication approach
Needs people, good listener, status quo, dislikes change, no risks, no pressure, counsellor, helps others, questioning, insecure, needs reassurance, supportive and no conflict	Start with a personal commitment
	Be agreeable
	Show interest in them as people
	Listen well
	Be supportive and responsive
	Elicit personal goals
	Ask 'how' questions
	If you disagree look for hurt feelings
	Be informal, orderly and friendly
	Imply minimum risk
	Offer clear, specific results
	Offer guarantees

Analytical communication type	Communication approach
Planner, organiser, details, technicalities, slow decisions,	Be straightforward

must be right, conservative, cautious, low pressure, critical, problem solver, compliant and follows procedures	Be direct but low-key
	Stick to business
	List pros and cons
	Present specifics
	Take your time but be persistent; use step-by-step timetables
	Assure no surprises
	Document agreements for the record; formally present disagreements
	Be accurate and realistic
	Provide solid and tangible evidence
	Provide long-term guarantees

Activity

Activity 1.4a   30 minutes

How would you engage the support of each of these communication preferences in your financial proposal — both in written format and in a verbal presentation.

	Written proposal	Verbal presentation
Dominant		
Expressive		
Solid		
Analytical		

You need to be able to do all this in one report so how would you structure it overall to include all your ideas above.

1.5 Scenario planning

For an overview of different approaches to scenario planning read the checklist 'Using scenarios'.

For a financial proposal, scenarios are important in a number of ways:

- You can include different risk scenarios.

- You can look at alternative ways of achieving the same end — leasing versus purchasing decisions.

- You can model different product or market offerings.

- You can model different cost structures — fixed versus variable, outsource versus in-house.

Each of these will have an impact on the complexity of the proposal you're putting forward. It's a great skill to be able to show the reader without totally bemusing or switching most of them off that you've taken lots of possibilities into account.

One scenario often required is a worst-case scenario, although it can be difficult to ascertain what would actually be the worst case. Also, if you took the worst case for every variable in your plan, then it would be unlikely that you were modelling anything realistic.

1.6 Risk assessment

If you don't think of the problems someone else will! So the best technique is to show that you've thought of everything that could go wrong — and you've thought of what you could do to mitigate the risk and then applied a risk factor to the project.

Organisations often have an internal mechanism for doing this, which may be through an 'internal rate of return' (you'll look at this in Topic 2) or a commercial risk-scoring questionnaire.

An example of a risk analysis matrix looks like this. Gross risk is the risk before the application of any controls or mitigating actions. The net risk is the risk facing the department after the application of current controls. I stands for impact (how dramatic) and L stands for likelihood.

Risk no	Risks	Gross risk		How will you manage the risk?	Net risk		Is risk acceptable?
		I	L		I	L	Yes/No

For another example of a risk matrix, refer to the suggested resource.

For a full financial proposal you may need to identify the financial impact for some or all of these risks as part of the scenario planning.

An interesting issue is raised in Ruchala's article 'The Influence of Budget Goal Attainment on Risk Attitudes and Escalation'. It links some of the issues here with the behavioural issues raised in Section 2.

Activity

> **Activity 1.6a**   **30 minutes**
>
> Perform a risk analysis on a recent project in your organisation using the above method.
>
> Then critique this against the approach to risk analysis currently used in your organisation.

1.7   Selling the benefits

You may feel that so far this has seemed pretty negative — risk analysis, worst-case scenario. But a good business case has also got to state the benefits. This is often summarised in a cost—benefit analysis, although sometimes this suggests some sort of straight-line relationship between each of the costs and each of the benefits.

In a cost—benefit analysis you would simply list the advantages and disadvantages of the plan and try and put some financial values against each. This can be challenging as you try to look for a method to quantify what might at first seem unquantifiable. For an example see Johnson *et al.*, Chapter 10.

Supporting resources

Books

1   Atrill, P., and McLaney, E., 2007, *Management Accounting for Decision Makers*, FT Prentice Hall — although aimed at

students of management accounting, it does set the subject within a management framework, with some good visuals and practice exercises.

2 Rice, A., 2007, *Accounts Demystified — The Astonishingly Simple Guide to Accounting*, Prentice Hall — a good introduction based more on words than numbers and taking away any fear for those looking at finance for the first time.

3 Fitzgerald, R., 2002, *Business Finance for Managers: An Essential Guide to Planning Control and Decision Making*, Kogan Page — a comprehensive text book covering both management discussion and the figures.

4 Johnson, G., Scholes, K., and Whittington, R., 2008, *Exploring Corporate Strategy*, FT Prentice Hall — Chapter 10.

Articles

5 Ruchala, L.V., 1999, 'The Influence of Budget Goal Attainment on Risk Attitudes and Escalation', *Behavioral Research in Accounting*, Vol 1, pp. 161–90. **P+**

Checklists

6 Effective business writing. **P+**

7 Writing a business plan. **P+**

8 Using scenarios. **P+**

Document outlines

9 Business case. **P+**

10 Risk management document. **P+**

Multimedia

11 'Making a business case' in the *Principles of Project Management* e-learning module. **P+**

Weblinks

12 www.berr.gov.uk/aboutus/corporate/projectcentre/

Topic 2: Analysing financial viability

Introduction

This topic provides you with the tools and techniques to analyse the financial viability of a project or expenditure proposal. The financial appraisal tools are cost–benefit analysis, breakeven analysis, payback analysis and discounted cashflow (sometimes called 'net present value'). You'll also review the cost of capital and a financial indicator called 'internal rate of return'. Finally, you'll see how to measure the inflows and outflows of cash.

2.1 The financial appraisal tools

Proposals for expenditure can be varied. Here are some examples:

- a simple, one-off small amount spend – to attend a management development programme

- a permanent increase to the fixed costs – to employ an extra management accountant

- a fixed duration project with income or expense implications – to tender for a three-year government contract

- a major item of capital expenditure – to invest in a new kidney dialysis unit, which will almost inevitably also have an impact on income and costs

- the implementation of strategic change – office relocation to new premises.

The expectation of you as a senior manager is to know which financial-appraisal tools to use in each of these cases. You need a simple way of understanding the impact of what you're asking for in terms of additional revenue spend.

You need to put together a profit and loss statement or balance sheet to support your proposal. You're going to concentrate on looking at financial-appraisal tools and on estimating the implications of the expenditure compared with other uses for that money. You also need to think about how the organisation's financial performance will look after the investment, both through some ratios and key financial indicators.

Capital expenditure tools basically rely on simple and sensible cashflow forecasting and yet have become regarded as something of a black art. Many textbooks concentrate on the black art without emphasising the fact that without a decent cashflow forecast any application of a capital appraisal tool is going to be building on shifting sand.

 For a brief introduction to investment appraisal see the checklist 'Investment appraisal'. For a more detailed look refer to Atrill and McLaney's *Management Accounting for Decision Makers*.

Cost—benefit analysis

Cost—benefit analysis (CBA) is used for both capital investment appraisal and revenue expenditure. A simple CBA looks at the direct and indirect costs, which are relatively simple, and then tries to quantify the benefits — which are not so simple.

CBA is more popular in the public sector. In its simple form, it's carried out using only financial costs and financial benefits. For example, a simple cost—benefit ratio for a road scheme would measure the cost of building the road and subtract this from the economic benefit of improving transport links. It would not measure either the cost of environmental damage or the benefit of quicker and easier travel to work. A more sophisticated approach to building a cost—benefit model is to try to put a financial value on these intangible costs and benefits.

For more information on cost—benefit analysis refer to Jones and Pendlebury's book *Public Sector Accounting*.

Breakeven analysis

If you are in a private sector organisation, understanding the meaning of gross profit and its implication on project breakeven can be helpful.

The impact of a one-off additional revenue spend can be looked at simply by using a quick formula:

$$\text{Additional sales needed} = \frac{\text{Cost of the additional expenditure}}{\text{Gross profit \%}}$$

Comparing these in different organisations, a £50,000 extra overhead spend would require the following.

Gross profit %	30%	40%	50%	60%
Additional sales needed	166,667	125,000	100,000	83,333

This would only make the same net profit as before and your net profit percentage will be less.

Most projects involve both direct or variable costs and indirect or fixed costs. Breakeven analysis builds in the complexity of both of these and allows you to estimate the volume at which the project breaks even. It even allows you to see how much money you're losing at lower volumes and how much money you could make at higher volumes.

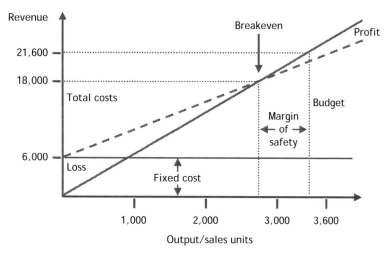

Figure 2.1a: A breakeven analysis

 For more information on breakeven analysis, refer to Atrill and McLaney's *Management Accounting for Decision Makers*.

Payback analysis

The most simple capital appraisal tool is the payback analysis. Payback analysis measures the cashflows associated with a project to assess how long it takes for an investment to generate sufficient cash to recover in full its original capital outlay.

To calculate the payback, a cashflow projection would need to be prepared estimating the additional cash inflows and outflows associated with the new investment. This should include the original cost of any fixed assets.

Here is an example. Imagine you have a choice between two machines.

Net cash inflows	Machine A	Machine B
Original cost	£40,000	£60,000
Year 1	£20,000	£20,000
Year 2	£15,000	£20,000
Year 3	£10,000	£20,000

 Machine A pays back faster — in 2½ years. Payback analysis would say you always take the project that pays back fastest as this is least risky and gives you your cash back most quickly to reinvest in another venture. This may be a good approach when operating in a market with rapidly changing products or technology. (See Fitzgerald's *Business for Finance Managers* for a discussion on this.) If an organisation has limited funds there may be more projects than free resources, and capital rationing will result. Quick payback helps reduce such capital shortages.

Although not considered to be a leading-edge capital-appraisal tool, payback analysis does keep coming back into fashion, especially in unpredictable markets and risk averse organisations.

But you must also recognise its limitations. Payback does not do the following:

- consider continuing cashflows
- take into account the future value of money.

It also only considers projects in isolation and doesn't examine the overall benefit to the company of the investment — or how the money could have been better spent elsewhere.

Discounted cashflow and net present values

Discounted cashflow is used to calculate the future value of money. If you were offered an investment that promised to pay you £100,000 in ten years' time what does that mean in today's money?

This now gets more complicated and involves using the technique of discounting. But, help is at hand in the form of the discount tables or even built-in formulae in spreadsheets. All you have to know is the following:

- how long the project will last
- the cost of the capital.

Here is a discount table. i = the cost of the capital (discount rate) and n = the length of the project in years.

Present value of £1 received after n years discounted at i%

n \ i	1	2	3	4	5	6	7	8	9	10
1	.9901	.9804	.9709	.9615	.9524	.9434	.9346	.9259	.9174	.9091
2	.9803	.9612	.9426	.9246	.9070	.8900	.8734	.8573	.8417	.8264
3	.9706	.9423	.9151	.8890	.8638	.8396	.8163	.7938	.7722	.7513
4	.9610	.9238	.8885	.8548	.8227	.7921	.7629	.7350	.7084	.6830
5	.9515	.9057	.8626	.8219	.7835	.7473	.7130	.6806	.6499	.6209
6	.9420	.8880	.8375	.7903	.7462	.7050	.6663	.6302	.5963	.5645
7	.9327	.8706	.8375	.7903	.7107	.6651	.6227	.5835	.5470	.5132
8	.9235	.8535	.8131	.7599	.6768	.6274	.5820	.5403	.5019	.4665
9	.9143	.8368	.7894	.7307	.6446	.5919	.5439	.5002	.4604	.4241
10	.9053	.8204	.7664	.7026	.6139	.5584	.5083	.4632	.4224	.3855

		11	12	13	14	15	16	17	18	19	20
	1	.9009	.8929	.8850	.8772	.8696	.8621	.8547	.8475	.8403	.8333
	2	.8116	.7929	.7831	.7695	.7561	.7432	.7305	.7182	.7062	.6944
	3	.7312	.7118	.6931	.6750	.6575	.6407	.6244	.6086	.5934	.5787
	4	.6587	.6355	.6133	.5921	.5718	.5523	.5337	.5158	.4987	.4823
n	5	.5935	.5674	.5428	.5194	.4972	.4761	.4561	.4371	.4190	.4019
	6	.5346	.5066	.4803	.4556	.4323	.4104	.3910	.3704	.3521	.3349
	7	.4817	.4524	.4251	.3996	.3759	.3538	.3332	.3139	.2959	.2791
	8	.4339	.4039	.3762	.3506	.3269	.3050	.2849	.2660	.2487	.2326
	9	.3909	.3606	.3329	.3075	.2843	.2630	.2434	.2255	.2090	.1938
	10	.3522	.3220	.2946	.2597	.2472	.2267	.2080	.1911	.1756	.1615

	What happens	Why it happens
Note 1	As you move down the columns, the factors become smaller	You have to wait longer for your money
Note 2	As you move across the rows, the factors become smaller	As the cost of the capital increases, the present value of money in the future decreases

The formula to calculate the present value is as follows:

$$\text{Present value of future receipt(s)} = \text{Amount of each future receipt} \times \text{Factor for discount rate and waiting period (present value factor)}$$

Activity

Activity 2.1a   15 minutes

Practise using the discount table by finding out the present values of the following. The first two are given so you can check your understanding of the table.

Amount	Interest rate (I)	Number of years (n)	Discount factor	Present value
£1,600	5%	5	.7835	£1,254
£135,000	16%	2	.7432	£100,332
£84,000	12%	6		
£3,500	10%	10		
£67,834	4%	10		
£100,000	8%	5		
£100,000	12%	5		
£100,000	12%	10		

If you compare this with the 'payback' exercise used earlier, it will become clearer how the results have changed.

A 5 per cent cost of capital would be appropriate, and this has been chosen as the discount factor. Also taken into account are *all* the flows of money over the project, not just those needed for payback.

	Machine A			Machine B		
	Cashflow	Discount factor @ 5%	Present value	Cashflow	Discount factor @ 5%	Present value
Original cash spend Year 0	(£40,000)		(£40,000)	(£60,000)		(£60,000)
Net cash inflow						
Year 1	£20,000	.9524	£19,048	£20,000	.9524	£19,048
Year 2	£15,000	.9070	£13,605	£20,000	.9070	£18,140
Year 3	£10,000	.8638	£8,638	£20,000	.8638	£17,276
Year 4	£ 5,000	.8227	£4,114	£15,000	.8227	£12,341
Year 5	NIL	.7835	NIL	£10,000	.7835	£7,835
Total cash inflow	£50,000		£45,405	£85,000		£74,640
Net present value (NPV)	£10,000		£5,405	£25,000		£14,640

Machine B has the higher net present value and would therefore be the choice. Put simply, this means that the project makes more money in real terms and creates more cash to reinvest. This is the reverse of the decision that you would have made using payback.

The absolute rule of discounted cashflow is that if it creates a negative net present value, do not do it. You might just as well burn the cash now.

 The role and continuing acceptance of discounted cashflow as part of a range of financial and non-financial methods of securing funding for projects is discussed in Chen's article 'DCF Techniques and Non-financial Measures in Capital Budgeting'.

2.2   Cost of capital

So far there have just been vague references to the term 'cost of capital' without a real explanation. To keep this simple you need to consider:

- anticipated risk
- your own attitude to risk
- opportunity costs for that £1,000
- interest rates

■

■

Possible figure for cost of capital	When it may be appropriate

■

■

Internal rate of return (IRR)

Activity

Activity 2.2a	30 minutes

2.3　　Measuring inflows and outflows of cash

■ **Totally new venture:**

■ **Investing to make current operations more efficient:**

■ **Replacing an existing machine or computer system:**

Supporting resources

Books

Management Accounting for Decision Makers,

Public Sector Accounting,

Business Finance for Managers: An Essential Guide to Planning Control and Decision Making

Articles

fi

Behavioral Research in Accounting

P+

Checklists

P+

P+

Multimedia

Principles of Project Management   P+

Topic 3: Feeding back on the financial proposal

Introduction

- ■
- ■
- ■
- ■
- ■

3.1 Project prioritisation

- ■
- ■
- ■
- ■

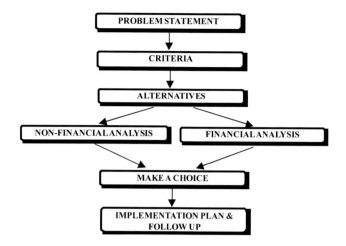

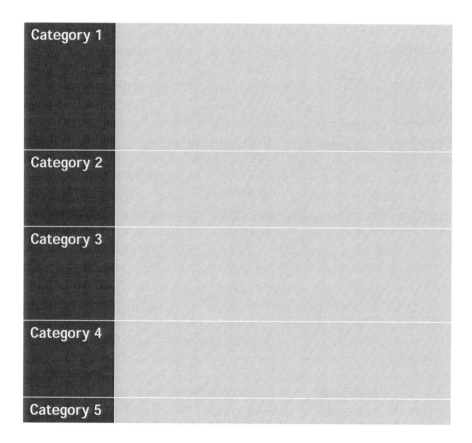

SR

3.2 Strengths and weaknesses analysis

	Strength	Weakness

3.3 Impact on organisational objectives

Objective	Weighting	Project 1 score	Project 2 score	Project 3 score
Total	100%			

3.4   Organisational risk

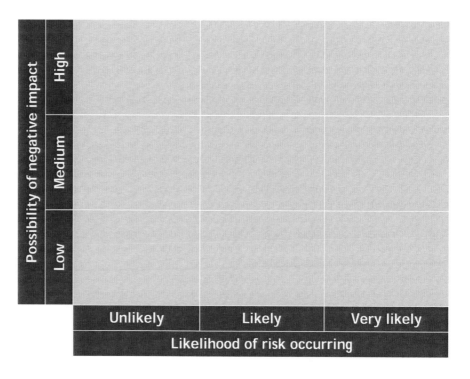

SR

Activity

Activity 3.4a	30 minutes

Criteria for targeting decisions for monitoring

-
-
-
-
-
-
-

Supporting resources

Weblinks

Section summary

Topic 1: Presenting financial proposals

-
-
-
-
-
-
-

Topic 2: Analysing financial viability

-
-
-

Topic 3: Feeding back on the financial proposal

-
-
-
-

Activity

Section summary activity	3 hours

-
-
-

Further reading

Public sector

Finance for Non-Financial Public Sector Managers

Finance and Accounting Guide for Not-for-Profit Organizations,

Not-for-Profit Accounting Made Easy

Private sector

Background

Financial Control

—

Accounts Demystified – the Astonishingly Simple Guide to Accounting

Detail

Management Accounting for Decision Makers,

Business Finance for Managers: An Essential Guide to Planning, Control and Decision Making

Before you move on

Preparing for assessment

Pathways Plus

The Management and Leadership Standards

How this development guide relates to the National Occupational Standards

Unit	Unit title	NOS units